The Great Belzoni

History's Indiana Jones

Travis "T.J." Frank

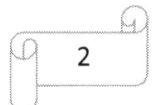

Contents

Ozymandias and the Giant....5

The Gentle Giant From Padua...17

The Patagonian Sampson....29

Journey to Egypt...44

The Showman Meets the Pharaoh....60

Belzoni Moves the Head....78

The 'Castle in the Air'....99

Belzoni The Archaeologist....116

The Next Adventure....129

Return to the Temple of the Sands....153

Return to the Valley of the Kings....175

Opening the Second Pyramid....203

Final Days in Egypt....228

Return to Europe....261

The Final Adventure....280

Legacy....289

Bibliography.... 307

Photo References....311

"Now I understand the man who build this. I don't know his name, but I know he's a real showman"

- Giovanni Belzoni (Egypt BBC: Temple of the Sands, 2005)

Ozymandias and The Giant

London, January 11th, 1818. A newsie is standing curbside waving newspapers around. "Extra, Extra, read all about…" As the cries of the young lad were drawn out from the thunderous clapping of horse-drawn carriages, a man came up and paid the newsie for a copy. The man hastily scanned the paper looking for something. On page twenty-four of the London Examiner's poetry section, the young man found his poem: *Ozymandias*.

The man slapped his hand on the paper and let out a huge shout for joy. "Ha! Looks like I won our little contest after all Horace!" He turns to the newsie and shook his shoulders. "Do you know what this means little one? It means MY Ozymandias got published before that buffoon Horace!" The newsie kicks him in the shin and storms off. Though in pain, the man was too excited. He tucked the paper under his arm and limped his way back to tell his beloved wife the great news.

While that was going on, his wife was busily reading a scary tale of next to the fireplace when she hears shouts from the other room. "Mary! Mary! Mary where are you!? I got some fantastic news!" Mary, with her soft grey eyes, rushed over to her husband. "What is it, Percy? What great news have you brought!?" Percy embracing her in his arms, I've done it, Mary! The London Examiner published Ozymandias before Horace's! I won the bet!" Mary shrieking for joy, hugs Percy tighter. "Oh Percy, my darling that's wonderful!" The young man whose poem graced the London Examiner's paper was the great Romantic poet, Percy Bysshe Shelley.

A year before Ozymandias' publication, Percy heard word that the British Museum had acquired an exquisite piece from the land of the Pharaohs: a colossi bust dubbed *The Younger Memnon*. But what intrigued Percy the most was the man who moved the Memnon: a seven-foot giant simply named Belzoni. Rumors began spreading like wildfire of how

Portrait of Percy Bysshe Shelly

Painted portrait of Mary Wollstonecraft Shelly. Today she is remembered for writing the most influential scientific novel of all time: Frankenstein or The Modern Prometheus (1818); which would go on to be adapted into the greatest horror film, Frankenstein (1931)

this Belzoni character was able to move the Memnon using nothing but his bare hands! Others say he lifted the bust with one hand and carried it over his right shoulder! Fascinated by the Memnon, in the winter of 1817, Percy, his wife Mary, and their friend Horace Smith discussed for hours about Egypt, the bust, and Belzoni.

    Horace, a poet himself, was spending his time with the Shelley's at their home in Marlow between March 1817 and December 1817. It was here, both men decided to have themselves a gentleman's competition: to keep the highly anticipated public waiting for the *Younger Memnon* to arrive, both should write a poem about the bust and see whose get published first. Percy won the competition, but what was Ozymandias about? Percy's Ozymandias is a fictional retelling of how Percy met a "traveler" who visited Egypt and came across the crumbling Ozymandias:

> *"I met a traveler from an antique land*
> *Who said—"Two vast and trunkless legs of stone Stand in the desert. . . . Near them, on the sand, Half sunk a shattered visage lies, whose frown, And wrinkled lip, and sneer of cold command, Tell that its sculptor well those passions read Which yet survive,*

*stamped on these lifeless things, The hand that
mocked them, and the heart that fed;
And on the pedestal, these words appear:
My name is Ozymandias, King of Kings;
Look on my Works, ye Mighty, and despair!
Nothing beside remains. Round the decay
Of that colossal Wreck, boundless and bare
The lone and level sands stretch far away."*

Today, Ozymandias is still considered one of Percy's greatest poems that continues to inspire poets and writers. The success of Ozymandias did leave an impact on the general populace. Even though they haven't gazed at the Memnon, the public couldn't get enough about Ozymandias! After numerous delays, Ozymandias finally arrived at the British Museum in 1821 for the people of Great Britain to gander at.

    Once the public received word of Ozymandias' arrival, they stormed the British Museum to see the colossi and the new Egyptian collection. When they reached the museum's Egyptian wing, the public was stunned to discover a bearded giant covered in outlandish garbs standing before Ozymandias with a

What was Romanticism Period?

From 1780 to 1832, British Romanticism was a major period in the history of English. The Romanticism Period exploded during the beginning stages of Great Britain's Industrial Revolution; where society began to undergo radical changes such as the rise of liberal movements, voicing radical ideas like universal suffrage, abolitionism, atheism, and Parliament reforms. These Romantic poets based their poems on the conviction of connecting with the organic growth of nature with human creativity as a force of passion and incredible imagination of like-minded individuals; however, Romanticism was more of a revolution of the poet's creativity and power their poem had on people.

Many of the Romantics argued radical ideas within their poems. As William Wordsworth put it they could *"choose incidents and situations from common life."* Romanticism also had the power to give a voice or justice to those who were abandoned by society such as the poor, industrial workers, children, the disabled, and even the elderly.

Though revered today as a horror writer, Edgar Allan Poe was indeed a Romantic poet. He used the supernatural and macabre to explore the darker side of Romanticism; with his most famous being The Telltale Heart and the Raven.

George Gordon Byron or known by his royal visage, Lord Byron, was a Romantic poet and friend to the Shellys; who would be instrumental in helping bring Mary's masterpiece to life in the wet summer of 186

The colossi bust of the Younger Memnon or 'Ozymandias'. Residing in the British Museum, Ozymandias would play a key role in the life of Belzoni.

big smile on his face; as Ozymandias smiled back at him. Some gasped, others fainted, but others knew who it was. "Hey! I know you. You're the Great Belzoni! The Patagonian Sampson who could lift one hundred people with one arm while lifting a cannon off its muzzle with the other!" Belzoni chuckled. "I believe you are mistaken, my good sir. I can only lift two hundred people on one arm and lift the cannon with my pinky." Everyone laughed as he wiggled his pinky finger. He motioned his hand to the people. "With introductions out of the way, I would like to introduce you to my good friend, Ozymandias. See how happy Ozymandias you are making him feel." The crowd chuckling once more made their way to Ozymandias.

As they stared at the large colossus, Belzoni, with his boisterous personality, began recounting his time with Ozymandias. "There I was, moving the head of Ozymandias when I was attacked by one of the workers!" This got everyone's attention. They gathered around the giant as Belzoni began retelling his adventures in Egypt to the visitors; how he fought off bandits with nothing more than a whip, had to deal with French, and unearthing a magnificent temple choked by an ocean of sand using nothing but a water bucket. On that day, everyone was more enthralled by Belzoni's stories rather than

Drawn and painted sketch of the adventurer, Giovanni Belzoni in Egypt. Behind him are the Pyramids of Giza as he sports Arabic garbs and a long beard.

Ozymandias himself, but the life Giovanni Belzoni lived was truly out of an adventure story.

Chapter I

The Gentle Giant From Padua

    The man who would become the *'The Great Belzoni'* was born Giovanni Battista Bolzon on November 5th, 1778, in the Republic of Venice (modern Italy) town of Padua. Padua is known for its rich Byzantine domed architecture with each street corner having the finest cafes in the city. The Bolzon family, originally from Rome, was poor. Giovanni's father was a barber who spends his days cutting hair, shaving and trimming beards; scratching enough money to feed his fourteen growing children.

    Growing up, Giovanni's father wanted his son to follow in his footsteps as a barber, but at a young age, Giovanni didn't care for cutting hair like his father. He was more interested in the outside world. The young Bolzon, when he wasn't in school, would

Paduan botanical garden with Basilica in the background

stop by at the local cafes and hear old maritime stories from returning sailors of the outside world who may have or not been involved in piracy! Giovanni enjoyed listening to these stories, but Giovanni's favorite story was the then translated adventure novel *Robinson Crusoe* which fueled Giovanni's imagination of traveling foreign lands just waiting to be explored.

    Giovanni believed it was his destiny to not become a barber like his father, but be an adventurer like his hero, Robinson Crusoe. Giovanni's first call to adventure came when he was thirteen years old. One morning in 1791, Giovanni took his little brother Antonio on an adventure to Rome to "seek their fortunes". Giovanni, or *'Gio Batta'* as Antonio called him, walked several miles not knowing if they were heading for Rome until they were stopped by a merchant. The merchant happened to be traveling to the small town of Ferrara, and seeing the two Bolozon brothers exhausted, invited them to accompany him to Ferrara. The merchant even went as far as allowing Gio Batta and Antonio to eat lunch with him consisting of cheese, bread, and fruits.

    When they arrived at Ferrara, the merchant allowed the Bolzon brothers to take their lodgings in his quarters. In the morning, the merchant had to leave the Bolzon brothers due to a business appointment he couldn't miss. After parting on good terms with the merchant, Gio Batta and Antonio continued with their adventure to Rome. This was the first good luck the young Gio Batta would enjoy; however, their next encounter would be a nightmare for the two brothers.

What was Robinson Crusoe?

The majority of Giovanni's stories growing up came from maritime sailors and the adventure novel Robinson Crusoe. Written in 1719, by author Daniel Defoe, Robinson Crusoe tells the story of Robinson Crusoe, a man who, defying his parent's advice, and left his comfort living life in England for the open seas. On his first adventure at sea, Crusoe nearly dies; his second brings him great fortunes and the title of a merchant. On his third voyage, to Africa, he is captured and sold into slavery by pirates. Crusoe escapes and makes his way to Brazil where he becomes a wealthy plantation owner.

On a voyage once again to Africa to personally collect new slaves for his plantation, Crusoe's ship gets caught in a deadly storm and sinks leaving Crusoe as the only survivor as he washes on a deserted island. Salvaging what was left of his ship, Crusoe makes a life for himself on the island: interacting with the animals, hunting, and fishing, in tune with nature writing in his journal, reconnecting with his faith, fighting off mutineers, war captives, and even cannibals for the next 28 years until his rescue. The story of Robinson Crusoe, though fictional, is based on the historical Scotsmen, Alexander Selkirk, who from 1704-1709 was stranded on the deserted island of Juan Fernandez; after being marooned by his captain and made a life for himself amongst nature. When he was discovered years later, Selkirk had adapted to his new home and even faced his dangers with wild animals and Spanish sailors! After returning to the civilized world in 1709, Selkirk returned to the open seas as a privateer in the British navy but tragically died in 1721 from Yellow Fever. His body was buried at sea; however, his legacy lives on for future generations through Robinson Crusoe.

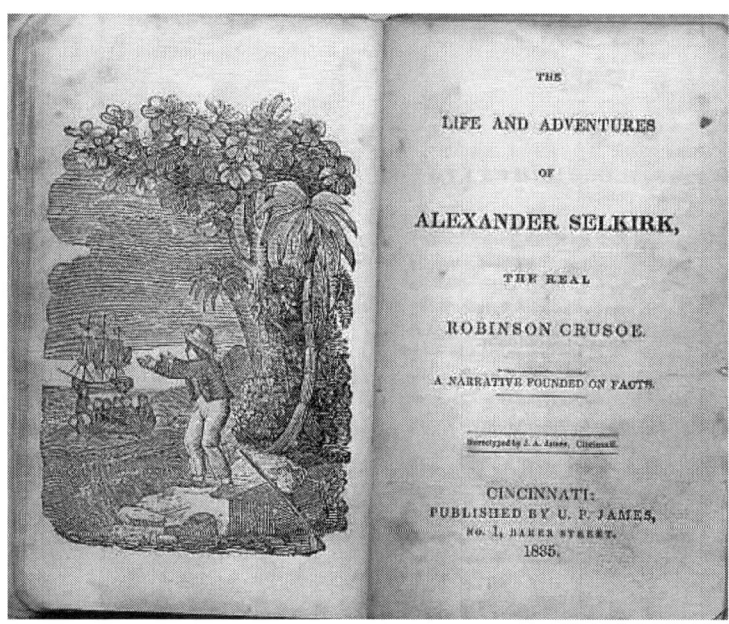

"The Life and Adventures of Alexander Selkirk. The Real Robinson Crusoe."

As they continued their journey to Rome, they happened to come across a carriage. They asked the resting *vetturino* (carriage driver) to give them a ride. After entering the vacated carriage, the vetturino demanded money from the Bolozn brothers, but when they explained they didn't have any, the vetturino aggressively ripped clothes off the Bolzon brother's back as proper payment. Instead of giving them a ride, the vetturino left the Bolzon brothers naked and penniless on the side of the road!

This kind of treatment would leave anyone shaken, but not Gio Batta. He saw this as nearly escaping from the clutches of death like his hero, Robinson Crusoe, and a minor setback. That night, Gio Batta and Antonio made it to a local town and huddled in each other's arms, shivering under a local doorway till the next morning.

With no money or clothes, the Bolzon brothers had to beg for their food and with little money, they gained, used it to get back home to Padua. In his first adventure, Gio Batta believed he made it to Rome but only made it as far as the town of Bologna. Despite his first adventure as an explorer ended unceremoniously short, Gio Batta continued to dream of adventure.

Three years later, the now sixteen-year-old Giovanni decided to seek out to Rome for a second time and this time around went off without any setbacks and made it to the eternal city. Before he left for Rome, Gio Batta's father implored him to learn the craft in case he couldn't find a suitable job. Yes, Gio Batta's dream came true after all, but since he had no means to sustain himself financially, he had to take up the one practice he refused: Giovanni was about to become a barber

    Though he hated the prospect of becoming a barber, Gio Batta reluctantly accepted his fate as a lowly barber. Now as a barber, Giovanni spends his days at his barbershop doing the mundane task of cutting hair, trimming, and shaving beards. He earned a small salary he could live on, but to his utter dismay, he was talented at this trade.

    It was during this time of mediocrity, Giovanni became fascinated with the new science sweeping across Europe known as hydraulic engineering; however, due to his time being preoccupied with the mundane task of cutting hair, Gio Batta didn't have the time nor resources to put this into practice. Two years into his apprenticeship, the now eighteen-year-old, Gio Batta fell head over heels in love with a

Nikolaos Gyzis "*The Barber*." Like his father, Giovanni would cut hair, shave and trim beards; a profession the young Gio Batta desperately wanted to avoid

young girl, but it wasn't reciprocated. The girl with whom he was in love with, harshly dumped him for his wealthy rival who could provide everything she desires. The breakup devastated Giovanni so much he decided to renounce his job as a barber, and take up religious vows, and become a Capuchin monk.

Gio Batta, now living a simpler life, was able to put into practice his love and knowledge of hydraulic engineering. He planned and constructed suitable wells and irrigation systems for the convent. Although the convent life allowed Gio Batta to pursue his passion for hydraulics, his spirit was restless and the call to adventure was too strong to ignore. Gio Batta felt like he outgrew the convent life both figuratively and physically.

By this time in his life, Giovanni had grown to a six-foot-seven giant and had the frame and strength of an ox. Gio Batta's time as a monk came to an end not by his own accord, but due to invasion. In 1798, Napoleon Bonaparte invaded Italy and ordered the dissolving of all religious orders including Giovanni's convent. Without a home, Gio Batta, not wanting to go back to shaving beards for the rest of his life decided to join the army. To dodge being forcefully conscripted to Napoleon's forces, Gio Batta decided to join the Prussian army. Joining the army

Portrait of a Capuchin monk. Gio Batta would've taken up the brown robe and practice monastic life for a few years.

may have been a downer for some, but for Gio Batta, it was the call his restless soul very much needed. Now in the Prussian army, Gio Batta was able to do the one thing he wanted to do since he was a child: to travel out from the confines of his native Italy and into the wider world. Gio Batta's life was about to take an unprecedented turn.

Chapter 2

The Patagonian Sampson

Now in the Prussian army, Gio Batta traveled across the European continent. During his tour across Europe, Gio Batta and his army compatriots would stop by the country fairs on their time off. When the public took one glance at the giant Gio Batta, they wanted to pay him to do feats of strength! Each time he went to a fair, he was asked the same question. This made Giovanni popular at county fairs despite not being part of the show.

At a fair in Germany, Gio Batta encountered a traveling troupe and stopped to watch the troupe's strongman performing herculean acts. One of the strongman's favorite acts was the "human pyramid" where he stood as the pyramid's base and carried as many as eleven men! Another favorite was the "sturdy table." The strongman takes two chairs, placing one at the end of his feet and the other under his head, while an anvil was placed on his chest. From there, two performers began banging away on the anvil making entire horseshoes on his chest! One lucky audience member was able to take home one of these horseshoes as a souvenir.

It was also during his time in the army where Gio Batta successfully further honed his skills in hydraulics. He utilized his hydraulic skills by putting on small shows of magic lanterns and musical lanterns. Gio Batta would be underneath the stage moving nodules around as water pumped through the pipes to make water dance across the stage and contort them to geometric shapes. Despite being a "one-man show" his shows were successful with the public and made a nice profit with each show; more than he made when he was a barber. Though he did get annoyed when the water either poured buckets from the pipes or the pipes was on the fritz, but was happy nonetheless.

At the dawn of the nineteenth century, Napoleon had returned from his expedition in Egypt, and Gio Batta had left the army and, using funds he

The Bonaparte Expeditions

While Gio Batta was traveling with the Prussian army, Napoleon Bonaparte was busy in Egypt. Egypt in the 18th century was closed off from Europe. At the time, those who knew and learned about Egypt came from the Bible's Old Testament. In July 1798, Napoleon and his forces invaded Egypt under the guise of liberating the country from their Turkish overlords, becoming the first to open Egypt to Europe in centuries. However, this was a ploy to capture Suez and create a canal that would grant France access to the rich markets of India and Africa.

Napoleon hoped to cut off their enemy, the British, from accessing their colonies and in the long term, invade their territories through civil unrest. Before he left, he commissioned the *Commission de Sciences et Arts d'Egypte's* 160 savants (scholars) to record Egypt's ancient and current history.

This would be known as the Bonaparte Expeditions For the next three years, Napoleon forces fought and were defeated by the British and their Turkish allies, but as that was going on, Dominique

Napoleon Bonaparte (on horseback) before the Sphinx

monuments. In 1802, Denon published his *Voyage dans la Basse et la Haute Egypte* (Journey in Lower and Upper Egypt), but the greatest legacy of the Bonaparte Expedition was the *Description de l'Egypte* (Description of Egypt). This landmark book contained massive and beautifully colored drawings of Egypt's ancient monuments, its geography, and a new map. This book would become the most popular book in Europe and created a craze for all Egyptians known as Egypt mania.

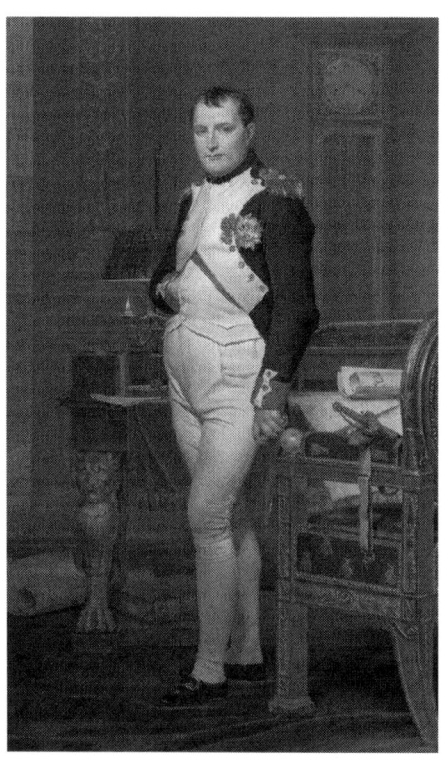

Painted portrait of Napoleon Bonaparte in his studies. Painted by Jacques Louis David 1812

received through his water shows, made his way to the Netherlands. Unfortunately, he wouldn't stay there for long. At one of his shows when Gio Batta had a slight misunderstanding with some French soldiers who had attended the show. To this day, it's unclear what this misunderstanding was, but what is known is Gio Batta struck one of the soldiers. Back in

Portrait of a Gio Batta during his tenure in Great Britain

the nineteenth century, striking a soldier meant prison time.

Gio Batta knew this upon his enlistment with the Prussians and the only way to escape this fate was deserting the army. Gio Batta fled from the army and made his way to Great Britain in 1803. When he arrived in Great Britain, Gio Batta decided to return using his birth name and went as far as changing his last name from *'Bolzon'* to *'Belzoni'*. Why did Giovanni change his last name to Belzoni? His surname Bolzon sounded like Spanish to the British people's ears.

During this time, the British were at war with Napoleon and their ally Spain and he could be mistaken for a Spanish spy. It was better to change his last name as a new fresh start in what would become his home for the next decade. Life in Great Britain seemed to be rewarding for the Giovanni. He met, fell deeply in love with, and married his true love, Sarah Bane, but at the same time a constant struggle. Giovanni continued performing his hydraulic shows with little to none fan fair. With little money to support Sarah, Giovanni was running out of ideas. Remembering his time in the Prussian army seeing the strongman's showman performance, Giovanni decided he would use his size and strength to transform himself into a worthy performer. On top of that, people would pay him to perform any herculean task they wanted.

Giovanni began performing on the streets and at fair booths showing off his strength and making decent money. It was during his performances he caught the eye of Sadler Wells, a known circus owner, and scooped up Belzoni for his troupe. On Easter 1803, Giovanni appeared before the public as the Great Belzoni. As the *'Italian Goliath'* in a recreation of *'Jack the Giant Killer'* or commonly referred to as *'Fee, Faw, Fum.'* It was here he began going by his signature moniker *'The Patagonian Sampson'* or the *'Roman Hercules'*. The headline read *'Signor Giovanni Battista Belzoni, the Patagonian Sampson will present extraordinary specimens of the Gymnastic Art perfectly foreign to any former exhibition."* This act being the human

The Story of Samson

In the Book of Judges, Samson was an Israelite judge known for feats of strength. When his father Manoah and his wife failed to conceive a child, an angel appeared before Manoah's wife to announce she would bear a son; whose destiny is to save the Israelites from their enemy the Philistines. The angel gave Manoah's wife one instruction: never cut the child's hair for which would become the child's power bestowed to him by God.

One of Samson's known feats was encountering a lion and ripping it apart with his bare hands! Days later, he returned to the spot where he slew the lion and saw a swarm of bees made a hive of the lion's corpse. Samson took some of the honey and ate it and at his wedding, asked his guests a riddle only he knew the answer to, and if they won would receive expensive robes for free. *"Out of the eater came something to eat/Out of the strong came something sweet."* The guests, unable to solve the riddle, asked his wife, who in turn gave them the answer. *"What is sweeter than honey? What is stronger than a lion.*" Angered by the betrayal, Samson went to Ashkelon and slew 30 men for their robes and gave them to the guests who answered the riddle correctly and left his wife.

Samson was known to have slain 1,000 men using nothing but the jaw bone of a donkey! Another was ripping the gates of Gaza straight off from its hinges. But Samson is known for his relationship with Delilah. After falling in love with Delilah, Delilah was visited by the Philistines who promised her 1,000 pieces of silver to find the source of Samson's godlike power. Delilah asks Samson what the source of his was power and after refusing to answer three times, he reluctantly tells her it's his hair. That night, as Samson slept in his bed, Delilah cuts off his hair as the Philistines arrived to take him, prisoner.

Now powerless for the first time in his life, was thrown into jail, but not before they beat him, chained him, and cut out his eyes. To celebrate their victory, the Philistines had a grand celebration and brought Samson out to humiliate him before their god, Dagon. Samson pleaded to God to give him

Lithograph of Samson, using his renewed strength, collapsed the pillars in the temple of Dagon taking the Philistines with him.

strength once more to get revenge on the Philistines one last time. With his strength restored, Samson grappled the temple's two middle column pillars (where he was chained to) threw all his weight against the columns until they collapsed; taking the temple, himself, and the Philistines down with him.

Sketch from one of Belzoni's shows. As the Great Belzoni, Giovanni is shown here carrying seven men with no assistance. That's how strong the giant from Padua truly was, no wires, no harnesses, just pure strength.

To put on a great act one must dress the part. During his tenure as a strongman, Belzoni every night would dress up either Samson or Hercules as he recreated their feats of strength before the ecstatic audience.

pyramid; in which Belzoni as the pyramid base walking around the stage carrying eleven grown men on a 127-pound iron-framed harness with nothing but his strength. Meanwhile, Sarah performed as cupid and stood at the top of the pyramid waving a tiny crimson flag.

Sadler even went as far as having Giovanni recreate all *'Twelve Labors of Hercules,'* straight out of the legends themselves. You can imagine the audience goers being amazed at Giovanni wresting a live lion on stage! Giovanni would juggle flags, lifting an entire cannon by its muzzle! His final act ended with him carrying seven grown men at one time with no assistance or devices. Giovanni, as a compromise with Sadler, was able to perform his magic lanterns display and water fountains.

Giovanni was, as one illustrated broadsheet put it *"he is in every way so perfectly formed that he is considered by artists as the finest model ever seen."* Giovanni spent the next nine years traveling across Great Britain performing his feats for the public.

After nine years of performing as a strongman on the British stage, Giovanni decided it was time to become a British citizen and in 1812 became a full citizen of Great Britain. In that same year, after traveling for years in Britain, the now thirty-four-year-old Belzoni made the choice to leave his adopted homeland left and venture out into the world. Giovanni took his act to Portugal, Spain, and Gibraltar, and other parts of Europe; however, in 1815, Giovanni once again became restless with life performing on stage as a strong showman and desired for adventure once again.

Chapter 3

Journey to Egypt

On the road, Giovanni continued to perform his magic shows, lifting people and cannons, but as time went on, he began to grow tired of showman life. What he wanted was a new challenge that would allow him to utilize his engineering skills. It was on a tour in Malta where he got his wish. In his off time from the stage, Belzoni heard word that the emissary for the Pasha of Egypt, Muhamad Ali, was looking for a hydraulic engineer. The Pasha had sent his emissary to the western world to look for new technologies to help develop his poverty-stricken country. The first way to do this was to create a suitable irrigation system to irrigate Egypt's deserts.

At a local café, Giovanni met the emissary, Captain Ishmael Gibraltar, and discussed hydraulics and the Pasha. Belzoni then offered his expertise to build a hydraulic machine that was easy, cheap to construct and would benefit the Pasha economically.

After lengthy negotiating with Ishmael, it was agreed that Giovanni should go to Egypt and present his plans before the Pasha himself. In May 1815, Giovanni, Sarah, and their teenage Irish servant, James Curtin, set sail to Egypt.

On the 9th of June, 1815, Giovanni, Sarah, and James arrived at the port of Alexandria. Unfortunately for the trio, as they entered the Hellenistic port, they received news the city was experiencing an outbreak of plague. Though uncommon today in Egypt, the plague was common back in the nineteenth century, but for Westerners, it was a death sentence. Due to the onset of the plague, the trio was forced to go into quarantine until the twenty-fourth.

> *"We were confined to our apartment, and for three or four days no one came near us. We were really sick, but I took the caution not to let it be known, for the plague is so dreadful a scourge, and operates so powerfully on human fears…"*

What is Hydraulics

      Hydraulics is the science of fluid mechanics and deals with the application of fluids in motion. Hydraulics primarily focuses on how water or other fluids flow in pipes, channels, dams, and tanks. The method of hydraulics began in 1650 when French scientist-philosopher Blaise Pascal and Swiss physicist Daniel Bernoulli created the laws that became the foundation of modern hydraulic engineering. The first law, Pascal's Law, proposes that all liquids moving in different directions are transmitted equally. The Second, Bernoulli's Law, states energy in fluids stems from pressure, elevation, motion, and if there is no loss in friction in either three, then the energy will remain constant. Five mechanisms push water through the pipes referred to as a hydraulic machine: the motor, the control valve, the pump, the driver, and finally the load. These tools allowed Giovanni to create and wow audiences with his magic fountain show he loved so much.

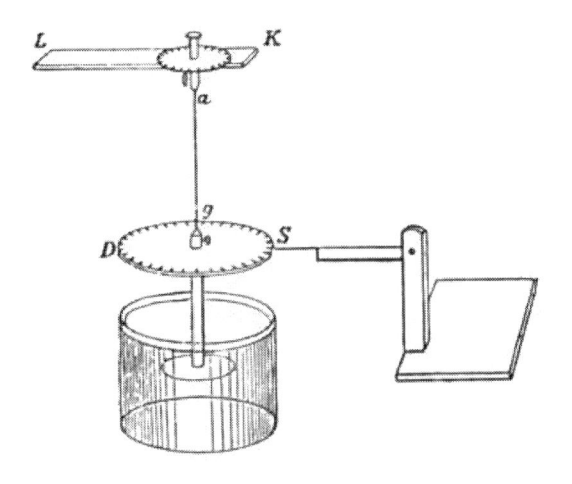

Sketch of a hydraulic machine

Once the twenty-fourth came and went, the plague ceased, Giovanni, Sarah, and James, set out for Cairo on the 1st of July 1815. Upon their arrival in Cairo, Giovanni met Mr. Baghos, the chief interpreter for Muhmad Ali and director of foreign affairs in Egypt, provided the three with a house to stay in while they are in the city.

    Though generous, the house was old, dilapidated, and barely furnished but this didn't stop Giovanni from site seeing. From where their new lodgings, Belzoni could see the Great Pyramids of

Giza calling out to him. The next day, Giovanni, Sarah, James, accompanied by Turkish bodyguards, went to visit the old monuments in the world. This was a moment Belzoni would never forget.

> *"I could not restrain myself from going to see the the wonder of the world, the pyramids...we went there to sleep that we might ascend the first pyramid early enough in the morning to see the rising of the sun and accordingly, we were on the top of it long before the dawn of the day. The the scene here is majestic and grand, far beyond description.: a mist over the plains of Egypt formed a veil, which ascended and vanished gradually as the sun rose and unveiled to the view of the smaller pyramids..."*

A few days later, Giovanni, alongside Mr. Baghos, traveled to the palace of Muhamad Ali, but as they were traveling, Giovanni was nearly killed! At this point, Egypt was one of the most dangerous countries in the world for any European. Although

Painting of the Giant Sphinx and Great Pyramids of Giza. Even with centuries being buried in sands and wore down, the Great Sphinx still stands as a testament to the ingenuity and craftsmanship of the Ancient Egyptians.

the Pasha welcomed "*Franks*" (Europeans), they were not seen favorably by the locals and ruling elite.

They feared their colonial ambitions would strip them of their power over the people. And they were right to be afraid. Both Great Britain and France wanted to spread their influence over the Pasha and its economy, but more importantly, raid as many ancient Egyptian artifacts from tombs or their temples. This was done to satisfy the growing demand from the public everything Egypt.

    Thus, the British, the Louvre Museums, and private collectors wanted to be the ones to have the biggest collections of Egyptian antiquities in the world. As Giovanni was traveling through Cairo on by donkey back, he came across a soldier who violently stuck him for being a European and this wouldn't be the last.

> *"We met a soldier on horseback, who, when he came near, gave me such a blow with his staff upon my right leg, that I thought he had cut it in two…After this he swore two or three oaths at me, and went on as if nothing had happened."*

This blow was so severe he not only was bleeding profusely but lost a large piece of his skin! Due to this unfortunate "accident," Giovanni was confined to his house in for thirty days to recover until he could

Muhamad Ali Pasha

Born on March 4th, 1769, Muhamad Ali in Kavala, a small Macedonian seaport off the coast of the Aegean Sea, and was a province of the Ottoman Empire. His father, Ibrahim Agha, was the local police chief and as a young boy was enlisted to the governor where he honed his political skills. Going by Mehmet Bey, Bey's Turkish origins, combined with his political skills from Kavala, he became a tobacco merchant before joining the Ottoman army. When Napoleon invaded Egypt in 1798, Egypt was another province of the Ottoman Empire and was ruled by the Mamluks. At the Battle of the Pyramids, Napoleon destroyed the Mamluk army.

For a time, Egypt was occupied by French forces British forces forced Napoleon to flee Egypt; leaving his men to continue to occupy Egypt until they had to withdraw from the country. This in turn left a power vacuum in the country. The sultan tried to reclaim control of Egypt, but due to political, civil disputes, and mutiny overpaid salaries resulted in losing control of the country. By this time, the young

Mehmet Bey was part of the Ottoman forces left in Egypt to oversee the city of Cairo.

He switched sides between the Mamluks and the Ottomans several times, but his main dream was to rule Egypt itself. The only problem was, the Mamluks had control of wealthy feudal land and it was their land that was the source of the country's wealth and power he needed to rest power from. using his political skills, and building his power base amongst village elders and wealthy merchants, he was able to appoint himself as the envoy of Cairo in 1805. In that same year, Ali launched a wide-scale attack on the Mamluks and succeeded in wiping them out and was "elected" as Egypt's Pasha.

Now that he was Pasha, Ali was free to pursue his agenda: to modernize Egypt. He did this by establishing cotton as Egypt's cash crop. This allowed Egypt to enter the modern world since cotton became a hot commodity in markets around the world. Ali went as far as forcing every farmer to grow and cultivate cotton and in turn, would be taken to textile manufactures and sold into the market. The

Nineteenth-Century painted portrait of Muhamad Ali, the Pasha of Egypt.

profits from the market would go directly to the country's treasury. But what Ali desired was to truly bring Egypt to the modern era. He sent envoys to the major powers in Europe to entice them to come to the country and allowed Europeans to visit Egypt and Cairo; making the country a popular tourist site for years to come.

stand again, but this ordeal left him a noticeable limp for a time. When he had fully recovered Giovanni was finally able to present to Muhamad Ali his schematics for his hydraulic machine. Ali did notice Belzoni's limp and would make sure those who harmed him were to be punished.

Giovanni, before the Pasha, proposed to him he would engineer a machine that would raise more water using only one ox than using four. But after he finished his proposal, the Pasha revealed the wheel he was inquiring about wasn't meant to irrigate Egypt's thirsty sands, but for fountains to feed his beautiful gardens at Soubra. Though dismayed by this revelation, Giovanni nonetheless took on the challenge.

Pleased with his proposal, Ali arranged for Giovanni to create his machine. As he was gathering his supplies for his hydraulic machine in Cairo, Giovanni nearly lost his life once more. When he was walking through the heavily packed streets, Pasha's troops began revolting against his rule and tried to overthrow him. They began attacking anyone who was on the streets especially those who were Franks. Giovanni barely made it to his quarters in time. The riots were hastily taken down by soldiers loyal to Ali and the traitors were executed for their crimes; to which Belzoni later regarded as barbaric for anyone to see.

    When the revolt was quashed, Giovanni resumed working on his hydraulic machine. He was given instructed orders to transport and present his machine at the Pasha's Soubra garden. Giovanni noticed during the construction of his machine, a discarded hydraulic machine. It was a gift from the English to Ali to help irrigate the "desert" but had since deemed a failure; due to the engineer not knowing Egypt's landscape and how much water needed to be drawn to irrigate the entire country. This failure served as a symbol of what Giovanni's fate would be if he failed and worked harder than he ever had up to this point.

    One day, Giovanni was traveling by donkey to Cairo to pick up a piece for his machine, when he

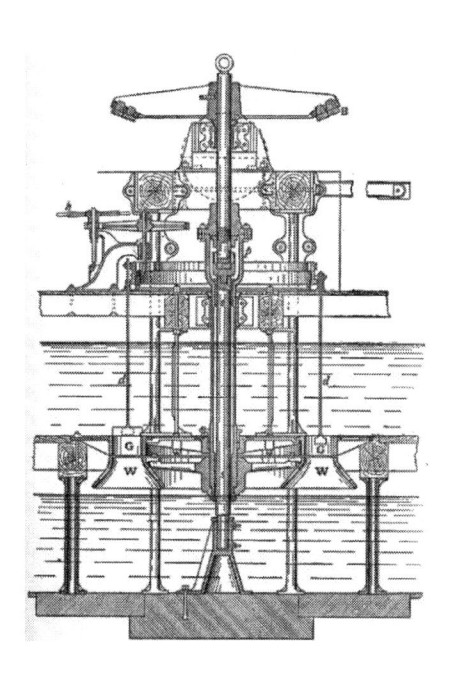

Schematics for a hydraulic machine

turned into the alleyway and was met by a *Binbashi* (subaltern officer) and his men. Giovanni recorded this day as the day *"which showed me plainly the country I was in, and the people I had to deal with."*

The officer approached Giovanni and tried to give him a devastating blow to the chest, only to bounce off from Giovanni as if he was a wall! In response to the officer's weak punch, Giovanni whipped his shoulders for good measure! *"Not being accustomed to putting up with such salutations, I returned the compliment with my whip across his naked shoulders."* But the stubborn officer wasn't done yet.

> *"Instantly, he took his pistol out of his belt, I jumped off my donkey, he retired about two yards, pulled the trigger, fired at my head, singed the hair near my right ear, and killed one of his own soldiers, who by this time, had come behind me. Finding that he had missed his aim, he took out a second pistol, but his own soldiers assailed and disarmed him."*

Luck appeared to be on Giovanni's side as he dodged another brush of death and these near-death experiences once more.

In the aftermath of the soldiers, Giovanni finally completed his machine. *"It was constructed on the principle of a crane with a walking wheel, in which a single ox, by its weight alone, could affect as much as four oxen employed in the machines of the country."* Upon completing his hydraulic machine, Giovanni presented before the Pasha and his Connoisseurs (experts in hydraulics) at Soubra. They had motives of their own to see this demonstration fail.

> *"The machine was set to work, and although constructed with bad wood and bad iron, and erected by Arabian carpenters and bricklayers, it was a question whether it did not draw six or seven times as much water as the common machines."*

After observing the power from Giovanni's machine, the Pasha was disappointed, claiming the machine drew as much as four oxen, but Giovanni's machine drew much as six oxen.

Ali decided to give Belzoni a second chance and ordered the ox to be removed from the wheel. He wanted to see *"by way of frolic"* if the machine would work with fifteen people at its helm; however no sooner was the ox removed, the wheel began to spin out of control. This was due to the wheel being the only thing keeping the machine perfectly balanced. The Connoisseurs stepped out leaving the young James, who got too close to the machine, being struck with such intensity, that it sent him flying until his body smacked the ground.

    The resulting velocity and impact broke one of his thighs; however, that wasn't even the worst of it. James got stuck in some of the machines lose parts and the machine was getting out of control. If not stopped in time, the young lad would lose his life. Seeing the machine was losing control, and James tangled up in the machine, Giovanni jumped right in and using his herculean strength, stopped the machine in its tracks! Despite saving the young lad, the connoisseurs saw these machinations of the machine as a bad omen for the country and not wanting to side with a Frank the Pasha condemned the machine as a failure. This failure devastated Giovanni and seemed to be the end of any prospects in Egypt.

Chapter 4

The Showman Meets the Pharaoh

During his final days in completing his hydraulic machine, Giovanni met a Swedish man named Johan Ludwig Burkhardt. It was in this meeting where Mr. Burkhardt told Giovanni about a *'castle in the air'* at a place called Ybsambul (modern Abu Simbel) in Nubia. Giovanni noticed how Burkhardt wore an Arabic dress and had a long beard. Burkhardt's reason was obvious: due to continual prejudice towards Europeans, Burkhardt adopted Arabic dress and grew out his beard to be more accepted as one of them and not seen as a "Frank." For the most part, it worked out quite well which Giovanni would take in for consideration.

In their conversation, Burkhardt told Giovanni about a colossi statue dubbed as the *Younger Memnon*. He lamented to Giovanni his desire to

Nineteenth-Century portrait of Johan Ludwig Burkhardt wearing Arabic garbs; while sporting a long beard to better accepted amongst the Arabic population. Giovanni would later adopt this motif in his travels in Egypt. 19th

remove the Younger Memnon from its resting place and present it to the British as a gift; however, many had tried and failed to move the Memnon including himself. Fascinated by this Younger Memnon and Burkhardt's other discoveries, Giovanni wanted to take part in removing the colossi bust for the British Museum. Burkhardt arranged a meeting for Belzoni to meet with his contact, the British Consul Henry Salt.

Henry Salt, the new British consul for Egypt had arrived where he met Mr. Burkhardt and discussed removing the Younger Memnon. In their conversation, Burkhardt mentioned Giovanni's interest in removing the bust. Salt remembered seeing Belzoni performing on stage as the Patagonian Samson and was dubious to talk to a showman about antiquities but was convinced by Burkhardt to hear him out. Giovanni met and explained to Salt he would be more than happy to undertake this challenge to remove the Younger Memnon and should go directly to the British Museum for the world to see; however, he lamented he needed to finish his hydraulic machine for the Pasha before he could move the Memnon.

After the disastrous ending of his presentation to the Pasha at Soubra, Giovanni was in a bind. He had used up his money to construct his hydraulic machine and barely had enough to leave the country but remembered his meeting with Mr. Salt about the removal of the Younger Memnon. Giovanni met with Mr. Salt once more and this time applied for the position. He recounted his story to Mr. Salt how his machine failed, was running low on money, and had an idea how to move the Memnon cost-effectively. By the end of their conversation, Mr. Salt was convinced Belzoni was the man he was looking for and accepted his application.

    Upon signing his one-year contract with Mr. Salt, Giovanni became an official employee of the British crown; however, the contract he signed didn't make him an employee for the British government, but with Henry Salt. Salt had his own eyes set on collecting and selling Egyptian artifacts himself. What better way to accumulate these artifacts than to have someone else do the dirty work for him. Several days later, on the 28th of June, 1816, Giovanni, alongside Sarah and James, set sailed from Cairo to the ancient Egyptian city known as Thebes. Thebes is three thousand miles south of Cairo. Before their arrival,

Salt personally gave Giovanni specific instructions to follow:

> 'Mr. Belzoni is requested to prepare the necessary implements, at Boolak, for the purpose of raising the head of the statue of the Younger Memnon, and carrying it down the Nile….[Mr. Belzoni] will spare no expense or trouble in getting it as speedily conveyed to the banks of the river as possible, and he will, if it be necessary, let it wait there till the river shall have attained sufficient height, before he attempts to get it into the boat….
>
> Mr. Belzoni will have the goodness to keep a separate account of the expenses incurred in this undertaking, which, as well as his other expenses, will gladly be reimbursed, as, from the knowledge of Mr. Belzoni's character, it is confidently believed they will be as reasonable as circumstances will allow…If Mr. Belzoni should ascertain the certainty of his being to accomplish his purpose, he is requested immediately to dispatch an express with the gratifying intelligence to Cairo.' -Henry Salt.

It was during a stay at Manfalut on the 5th of July, Giovanni met Ali's brother, Ibrahim (the leader of Upper Egypt) who offered the strongman advice to show his letter to the Defterdar (the local official) to gain the men needed for this endeavor. However, it was here where Giovanni met his future rival, ex-consul-general Bernardino Drovetti. Like Salt, Drovetti was collecting antiquities to sell off to the Louvre Museum. He was returning from his time at Thebes and had been raiding, collecting, and selling Egyptian artifacts for the French. He commended Giovanni's attempt to remove the colossi head of the Younger Memnon and confessed he had tried to move the head himself and failed to do so.

    To commemorate their new friendship, Drovetti offered Giovanni a granite cover sarcophagus he discovered in a tomb at Thebes and failed to remove from its tomb, but if Giovanni succeeded, it was all his. After their exchange, Giovanni returned to the Nile and set sailed to Thebes. On the 22nd of July, 1816, Giovanni and

Ramses the Great (1279-1213 BC)

As he embarked on to Thebes, Giovanni, nor anyone at the time knew the Younger Memnon was the statue of Egypt's greatest Pharaoh, Ramses II, or *'Ramses the Great.'* Ramses II came to power in 1279 BC, the son to the warrior king Seti I, and was the third pharaoh of the 19th Dynasty. In the early years of his reign, Ramses II recorded how the gods blessed him with good floods that provided a bountiful harvest for an ever-growing populace.

Like Belzoni, Ramses II too was a showman. From the beginning, Ramses II was determined his name would live on forever. The reason Ramses II is referred to as *'The Great'* is not due to him being a prodigious warrior king but as a monument builder. Ramses II would monument projects the likes of which since the building of the Great Pyramids. He had massive monuments constructed along the Nile and went as far as converting the temples of Thebes into monuments dedicated to himself.

He would take previous pharaoh's works and put his name over them as his own, but for his name to live on, he had it cut deeply not the rock. Incoming pharaohs would etch out their predecessor to legitimize their reign, but not for Ramses. No one was going to remove his name from history. With his flaming red hair, he left behind a memorable presence.

 The moment of his father's death, Ramses II made an impact on Egypt by going against tradition. It was the tradition for the upcoming pharaoh to not make any important decisions for seventy days (for the mummification process and the country to grieve for the loss of their pharaoh), but for Ramses II, he was too impatient. In his eyes, Ramses II wished to recapture the warrior visage of his predecessors, to show the world the Egyptian king was more powerful than any other king, to forge a new Egyptian Empire bigger than any pharaoh before him. The boisterous life of Ramses II would influence the life of Belzoni more than the adventurer could imagine.

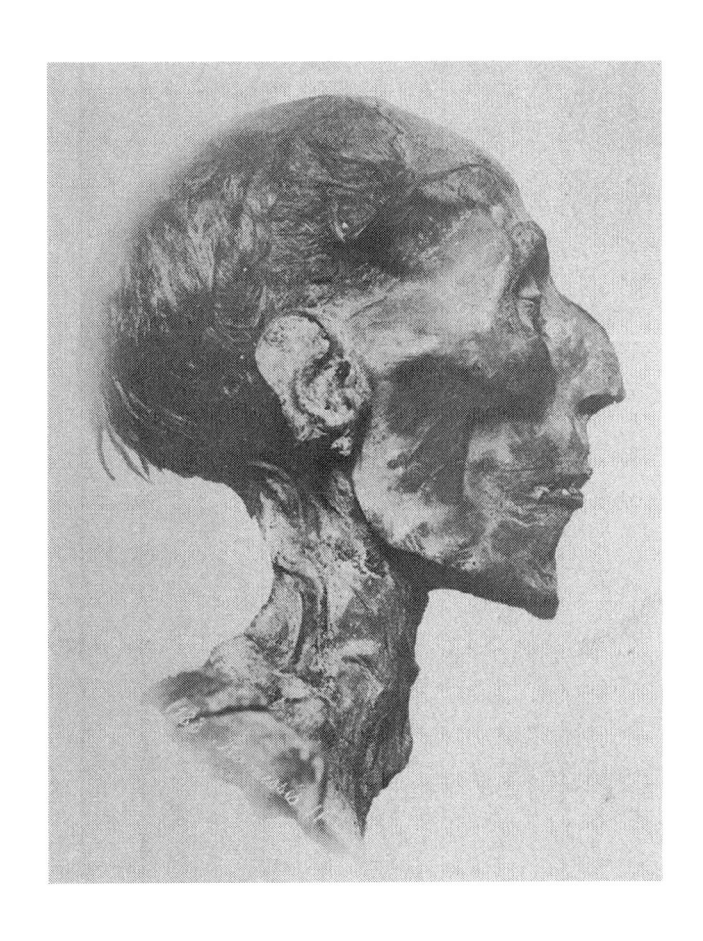

Side view of the mummy of Ramses II

Bernardino Drovetti, with his agents, resting his hand on a colossi head of a pharaoh. Drovetti would be a thorn in Belzoni's side during his tenure as an antique collector

his crew arrived at the ruins of Thebes (today's Luxor). Luxor was a town built on the ancient ruins of Egypt's center of religion. Here, they contained the rich legacy of Egypt's pharaohs. Giovanni made his way to the Younger Memnon, but to get to it he needed to pass an ancient temple called the Memnonium:

(top) Colonade pillars of Ramses II. (bottom) recreation of the temple.

71

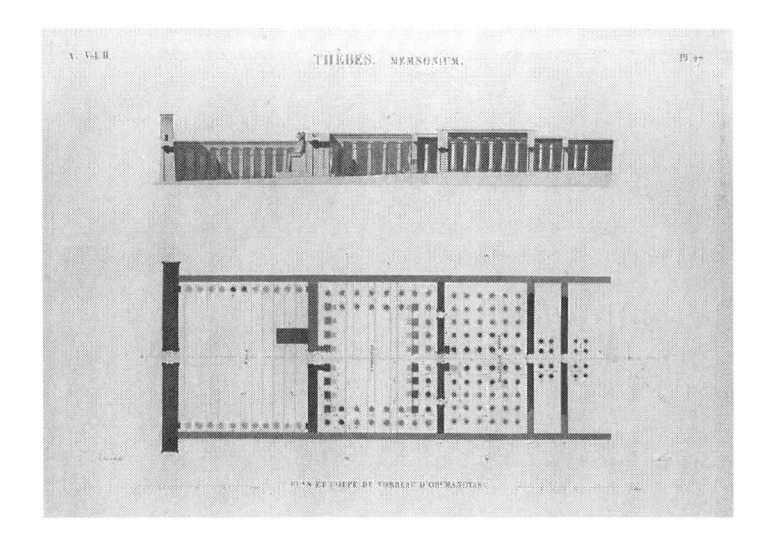

Schematic layout of the architecture of the Ramesseum.

Henry Salt

The man who would become the bane of Giovanni's success in Egypt was born on June 14th, 1780 in Lichfield, England. Son of a physician, Henry Salt grew up dreaming of becoming a portrait painter. In 1797, at the age of seventeen, Henry traveled to London and became an apprentice to artists Joseph Farington and John Hoppner, but in 1802, he decided to leave behind his dream of becoming a portrait painter.

Instead, he became the secretary and companion to Lord Valentina. From 1802-1806, Salt traveled with Lord Valentina to the Red Sea regions, the coast and interior of Ethiopia, India, around the Cape of Good Hope and Ceylon. Henry's talent as an artist served him well when Lord Valentina published his travels in three consecutive novels from 1802-1806 and tasked Salt to sketch and illustrate their travels.

Upon release, Salt's work was praised for its accurate recreations of monuments and ancient engravings. On his way back to England in 1806, Salt made a stop at Egypt where he met with the Pasha Mohamad Ali. His drawings of Egypt's ancient monuments made its way to Valentina's *Voyages and Travels to India*. In 1809, Salt traveled once again to Ethiopia on a mission from the British government to establish diplomacy and trade with Emperor Egwale Seon.

On his arrival, the Emperor was away and Salt decided to stay with his friend. It was here where Salt began to correct misinformation about Ethiopia from Scottish traveler, James Bruce. Due to his detailed observations and artistic skills, Salt earned himself a name within the British government and when it came time to elect the next consul to Egypt in 1815, Salt was chosen upon Valentina's recommendation. He landed in Alexandria in 1816 and made his way to Cairo where he began forming a good relationship with Ali and gain his approval to secure artifacts for the British Museum, but secretly was collecting for himself to sell off to private collectors.

Nineteenth-Century portrait of Henry Salt. Though business acquaintances now, Giovanni would grow to hate Salt for taking away his future accomplishments and making them his own.

" I had to pass before the two colossi figures in the plain. I need not say, that I was struck with wonder. They are mutilated indeed, but their enormous size strikes the mind with admiration….On my approaching these ruins, I was surprised at the sight of the great colossus of Memnon, or Sesostris, or Ozymandias, or Phamenoph, or perhaps some other king of Egypt.

This was Ramses' II memorial temple called the Rameseum. Known as the *'Mansion of Millions of Years,'* it was one of the largest temples ever constructed in Egypt. The Rameseum was Ramses II's plan to live for eternity. At the entrance to the temple were two pylons where they proclaimed Ramses II's successes as a builder and military leader.

    Amongst the walls were giant colossi statues of Ramses II. The temples pillared halls retell the story of creation with the columns acting as the first lands rising out of the universe's primordial waters. As he made his way out of the Rameseum, Giovanni located the colossi bust of Pharaoh Ramses II, but not in a good state:

> 'I found it near the remains of its body and chair, with its face upwards, and smiling on me, at the thought of being taken to England. I must say, that my expectations were exceeded by its beauty, but not by its size…I will not venture to assert who separated the bust from the rest of the body by an explosion, or by whom the bust had been turned face upwards'.

The bust was originally one large statue of Ramses II but was separated from an explosion. Years prior, the French had tried to move the colossi, but due to its eight-ton weight, it barely moved.

To make it easier for the French, they decided to make the statue smaller to carry and drilled a hole over the statue's upper right chest, loaded it with dynamite, and KABOOM! With the top half blown off, it should've been easier to move right? The French and even Drovetti tried everything to make the bust move but couldn't move the Younger Memnon and gave up. How was Belzoni going to remove the Younger Memnon while others had failed?

     Giovanni, having been prepped of the colossi's position and state through Burkhardt's observations, had brought with him from Cairo everything he needed. Belzoni had fourteen poles, eight of them to make a "car" to lay the colossi bust on, palm leaves to act as ropes, and four rollers for the cart to roll over. That night, standing from his makeshift house near the Memnonium. Belzoni charted a course to take the colossi to the edge of the Nile, but there was a problem. It was now summer, which meant the Nile was undergoing inundation known as *Akhet*. This is when the Nile completing floods the entire Egyptian plain and fertilizes the land. If Giovanni didn't act soon, the head would be buried for an entire year!

Chapter 5

Belzoni Moves the Head

On the 24th, Giovanni met with the Cacheff of Erments to issue the assistance of eighty *Fellahs* (locals) to move the large colossi; however, Belzoni faced an entirely new problem. Early on, Giovanni came to understand the only way to get the local rulers to comply with requests, you must provide them with a gift; whether you are European or local. These gifts were usually coffee, powder, guns, food, animals, and so on. In other words, through bribes and deception will your wishes be granted, but Giovanni didn't do this. He was told to show his permit to the Cacheff and the Cacheff must honor the request.

Since it was the season of Inundation, the locals were either occupied in the fields or getting ready for the floods. Giovanni argues there were many fellahs not doing anything and he was willing to pay them; only for the Cacheff to point out its impossible. *"[for] they would sooner starve than undertake a task so arduous as yours, since, to remove that stone, they must be helped by Mahomet, or they will never stir it the thickness of a thumb.*" To make matters worse for Giovanni, Ramadan was just around the corner and once it started, no fellah could be forced to work in the fields.

Even with these setbacks, Giovanni was determined to move the head even if he had to do it himself. He lets the Cacheff know he would offer anyone who was idle to work sufficient payment and hopes the Cacheff would honor his request. The Cacheff promises to honor Giovanni's request as soon as he could find fellahs in need of work.

The following morning, no men appeared. Giovanni stood by the Ramesseum waiting patiently for the fellahs the Cacheff promised him. Eventually, his patience ran out, and angrily stormed off to the Cacheff. This time around, Giovanni decided to present the Cacheff with gifts of powder and two pounds of coffee; in the hopes this time the Cacheff would honor his request. After receiving Belzoni's "generous" gifts, the Cacheff promised once more to send some men Giovanni requested the next day.

The following day came and went and again, no one came. Giovanni was patient enough to hold out for the Cacheff's word but now felt like he was being insulted. He once more set out to meet with the Cacheff, but instead of bringing gifts as the Cacheff had hoped for, instead of threatened the small man, he would write to the Caimakan about his refusal to honor his request and not doing his job. It appeared the threat worked and on the 27th of July, 1816, the Cacheff, at last, honored his request and Giovanni began his work to remove the colossi. At first, the workers believed the Younger Memnon could never be moved from where it laid, but quickly changed their tune when they saw the colossi beginning to move.

"By means of four levers, I raised the bust, so as to leave a vacancy under it, to introduce the car, and

after it was slowly lodged on this, I had the car raised in the front, with the bust on it, so as to get one of the rollers underneath. I then had the same operation performed at the back and the colossus was ready to be pulled up....

I caused it to be well secured on the car, and the ropes so placed that the power might be divided. I stationed men with levers at each side of the car, to assist occasionally, if the colossus should be inclined to turn to either side. In this manner, I kept it safe from falling. Lastly, I placed men in the front distributing them equally at the four ropes, while others were ready to change the rollers alternately..."

Despite demonstrating to the fellahs the possibility of moving the colossi bust, Giovanni faced stiff opposition. From the 28th-29th of July, the workers began to grow restless and exhausted in moving the head of Memnon.

Lithograph of Belzoni overseeing the Fellahs moving the Younger Memnon from its resting place at the Menonium. Sketched and painted by Giovanni Belzoni.

Egyptian Laborers and Techniques

At the time, Giovanni didn't realize the tools he was using to move the Younger Memnon was eerily similar to how the Ancient Egyptians moved large granite blocks. In those days, being a laborer was the worst job any Egyptian could ask for. A large number of Egypt's population worked as a laborer where they worked in the fields of wealthy farmers, acted as servants to the nobility, but were forced to work on public building projects or grand projects like the Rameseum or the Pyramids of Giza. These laborers, though doing all the back-breaking work, were paid little and due to their status, couldn't rise the social ladder.

Effectively, they were consigned to a life of work with no chance to make a better life for themselves or their family. As to how the Ancient Egyptian laborer was able to move granite stone without modern equipment is truly a miracle. What the laborers did was use levers and sleds to slide large granite stones, statues, and obelisks onto the sleds. Each man would tightly tie a rope around the

Exterior view of Thebes. Sketched and painted by Giovanni Belzoni.

block and pull the block forward; while there those back of the sled propelling the sled forward. To move one block could take as many as thirty men! Giovanni, whether he was aware of it or not, successfully recreated the Ancient Egyptian method of moving land transporting large stones in over three thousand years.

They decided to rebel against the giant Paduan. Thinking they can catch Giovanni by surprise, one of the workers drew a dagger and ran towards the giant to finish him, but Giovanni, coolly, waited for his approach and slapped the dagger out of his hands. What came next was truly astounding. After disarming the fellah, a now enraged Belzoni immediately grabbed his attacker by his feet, lifted him, and as if he was a giant club, and began swinging at the workers!

The next day, the workers, shaken by the sheer strength of Belzoni, returned and resumed their work. There would be no future rebellions. Despite being the first man to move the colossi bust in three thousand years, the tole of the Egyptian heat took its toll on Giovanni.

> *"From the great heat of the day, I was unwell at night, having never felt the sun so powerful before in my life. Being the hottest season, the air was inflamed, and even at night, the wind itself was extremely hot. The place I had chosen in the Memnonium was worse than any, as the whole*

mass of stones was so heated, that the hands could not be kept on it."

Over the next few days, Belzoni felt the life drained from Egypt's unforgiving heat until it took its toll and had to take some time to recover. Unfortunately for his servant, James, the heat took its toll, and was forced to return to Cairo for medical treatment.

From the 29th of July to the 4th of August, 1816, Belzoni was able to move the colossi nearly one thousand miles from its ancient resting place, but hit a snag trying to get the bust over a hill and hoped to get it over before the flood. And he had to act soon, the flood was just around the corner. On the 5th, the workers failed to show up. Giovanni was perplexed. Everything was going smoothly, why stop now? Unfortunately for Belzoni, word had spread of the head being moved and made its way to Drovetti.

Furious that a circus showman was able to move the head, let alone British, where he had failed, Drovetti decided to step in and thwart any more

Colossi statues columns of Pharaoh Ramses II at the Rameseum

Aerial view shot of the Ramesseum today. It truly was as magnificent and grand in its heyday

progress. Since Drovetti was in Egypt longer than Belzoni, he had incredible influence over the local rulers. He even had agents who answered only to him. Drovetti sent his agents to the Caimakan and forced him to stop Giovanni from moving the head any further.

With only the guard watching over the bust, Belzoni received word that the local Caimakan had issued a decree: every fellah, from this day forward,

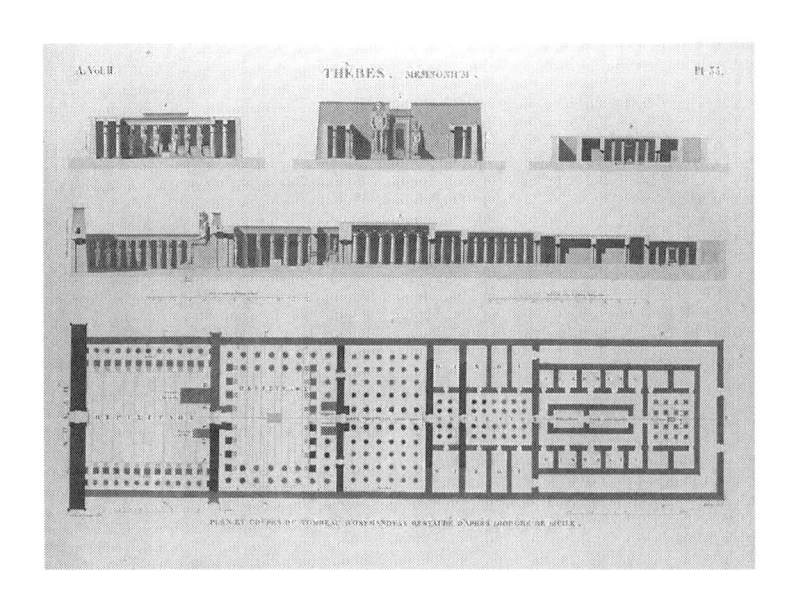

The entire layout of the Ramesseum

were to not work with any Frank any longer. As you can imagine, Giovanni, being so close to the edge of the Nile, was furious by this decree. *"It is to be observed, that the spot where the head lay at this time was expected to be underwater in a few days, and that by delay the risk would be incurred of having it sunk in the earth so that if couldn't have been taken out till the following year."* The flood was about to hit Egypt in a few days and if he didn't secure the bust in time, it would be another failure for him.

Giovanni, lamenting over the head being forced to stay put, sought to locate the Camiakan. He found him at his home in Luxor and wished to discuss continuing his operations. Throughout their conversation, the Camiakan was rude and disrespectful to Giovanni for being a Frank and wanted nothing to do with him. After being patient with the Caimakan's stubbornness, Giovanni had enough:

> *"My patience was great and I was determined that day to carry it to its utmost length, but there is a certain point, in which, if exceeded, these people do not understand and, in a country where respect is paid only to the strongest, advantage will always be taken of the weak."*

From their exchange, it became clear to Giovanni that being gentle wasn't going to get him anywhere. If anything were to get done in this country, he would need to be strong and not be bullied by those who are weaker than him; that respect is earned by the strongest and not the weak.

Then the conversation became even more heated. So heated, the Caimakan, like the fellah and soldiers before him, decided to seize this opportunity and attack the seven-foot giant:

> *"…he attempted to put his hands on me, which I resisted. He then became more violent and drew his sword, though he had a brace of pistols in his belt. There was no time to be lost, and I had received a good lesson in Cairo from another Albanian like himself, I gave him no leisure to execute his purpose. I instantly seized and disarmed him, placed my hands on his stomach, and made him sensible of my superiority, at least in strength, by keeping him firm in a corner of the room….*
>
> *The pistols and sword, which I had thrown on the ground was taken up by my Janizary, and after*

giving the fellow a good shaking, I took possession of them, and told him, that I should send them to Cairo, to show the Pasha in what manner his orders were respected."

Shaken by this event, the Camikan relented and allowed the fellahs to work on the 7th. By the 8th, the colossi bust was out of danger of being overtaken by the flood, but Giovanni couldn't celebrate just yet. On the 9th, Belzoni was struck with an intense case of heatstroke and had to cancel proceedings for the day. From the 10th-11th, the colossi head made its way to the bank. *"On the 10th and 11th, we approached towards the river, and on the 12th thank God, the Young Memnon arrived on the bank of the Nile."* After fifteen days and five miles of desert, the Younger Memnon made it to the bank and was ready to be shipped to Cairo then to Alexandria, and finally to the British Museum.

Despite the grueling heat and attempts at his life on two occasions, Belzoni came to appreciate how effective the fellahs were and argued they were

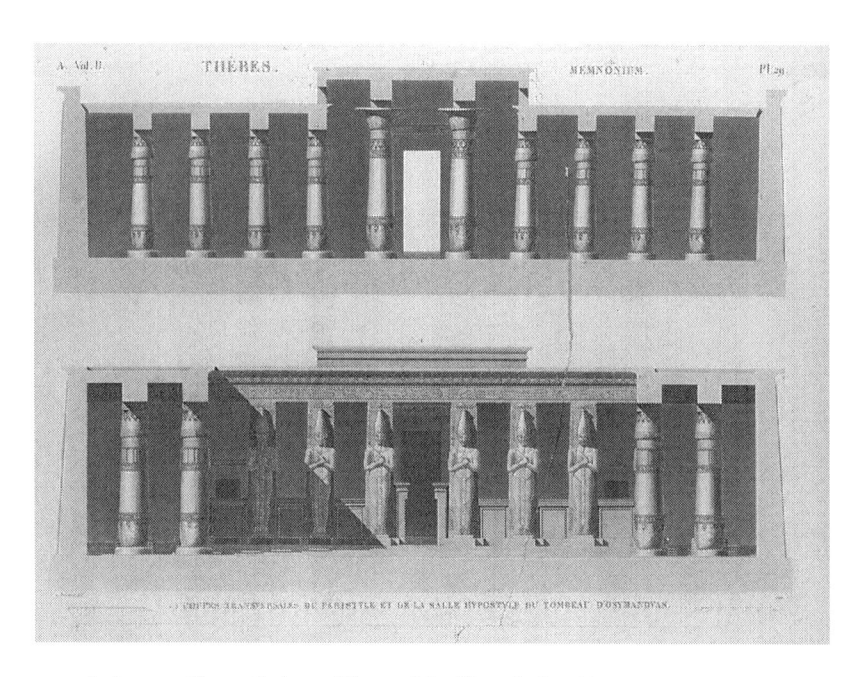

Schematics of the pillared halls of the Ramesseum

better than European workers. *"The hard task they had, to track such a weight, the heavy poles they were obliged to carry as levers, and the continual replacing the rollers, with the extreme heat and dust, were more than any European could have withstood...I am at a loss to conceive, how they existed in the middle of the day, at a work to which they were totally unaccustomed."*

To commemorate their hard work, Giovanni rewarded them with an extra piastre. This moment was a milestone for the adventurer. At this point, Belzoni felt like a failure, but now his adventurous spirit was rejuvenated, his confidence restored, and believe he can make something of himself in this country. For where the French, Burkhardt, and Drovetti had failed, Giovanni succeeded using only his wit, strength, and engineering skills. This would go down as Giovanni's first true success in Egypt and he was only getting started.

With his assignment now complete, Giovanni decided to take up on Drovetti's offer about the sarcophagus lid and decided to see if he could remove it himself. He asked the fellahs to take him to where the sarcophagus was located. They lead him to an open cave in the mountains of Gorunou and as he descended the cave with two fellahs and his interpreter, Belzoni came across the sarcophagus. *"I could not conceive how so large a sarcophagus, as it had been described to me, could have been taken through the aperture, which now the Arab pointed*

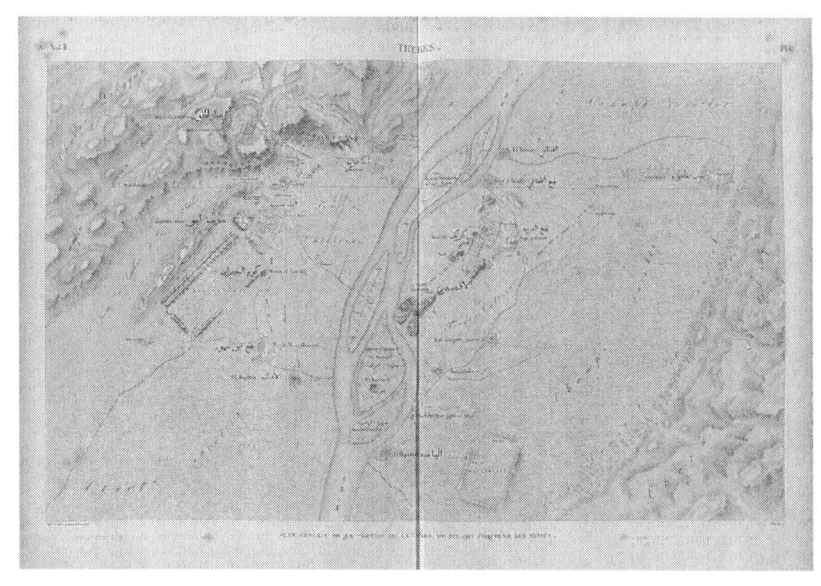

Open Map of the city of Thebes

Head of Pharaoh of Ramses II from the Ramesseum. Today, it resides at the Brooklyn Museum.

out." As he approached the sarcophagus, Belzoni had to step over scattered skulls and bone remains, but due to the narrowness of the tomb and his giant frame, he could barely fit.

He then heard a noise from his interpreter, and then nothing. Belzoni became impatient and decided to return outside, but when he asked one of the locals to lead him back out, the man didn't know. Due to this unfortunate circumstance, Giovanni had

More schematics of the Ramesseum with the herculean seated statue of Ramses II

to traverse the labyrinth-like chamber- placing markers on chambers- and he had to do it quick; the candle he held when he entered the cave nearly exhausted its flame! Eventually, Belzoni was able to find the entrance to the cave just as his candle blew out. It wasn't until he got outside, that his interpreter relayed to him how upon entering the passage, the Fellah fell into a pit that they didn't see and put out both candles; however, he found a small opening within the tomb and using his bare hands, created a bigger hole large enough for him to escape.

    Once outside, Giovanni discovered there was another passage much closer to the sarcophagus to remove it without damaging the lid. Belzoni had the trapped Fellah. The Fellah, upon his descent, broke his hip so badly he had a limp for the remainder of his life. From there, he successfully removed the lid of the sarcophagus. Giovanni once more, removed another piece Drovetti had failed to remove and Drovetti, hearing the word of this accomplishment, was of course angry, but couldn't do anything about it; since he promised the lid to Belzoni if he could move it and he did. It appeared now fortune was smiling upon the giant and it was only the beginning of what would become an adventure of a lifetime.

Chapter 6

The Castle in the Air

After successfully removing the lid from its tomb, Giovanni had a guard placed to watch over both the lid and the bust from vandalism. With his job completed, Belzoni had a lot of time on his hands and felt the winds of adventure calling out to him. Giovanni decided to follow up on Burkhardt's story of the *'castle in the air'* in Nubia and see if he could open the castle himself. Belzoni would go where few European men at that time had dared to explore. With Sarah at his side, Belzoni set sail to Nubia on the 18th of August 1816.

Giovanni and Sarah set sailed from Luxor to Nubia; a journey wrought with uncertainty and danger. They had no idea what to expect since no European man nor woman had ever ventured far up the Nile. Along the bank, they passed vast temples buried beneath oceans of sand. Giovanni made stops at these temples.

"On the 19th, we arrived at Esne. It's beautiful variety and fine shaped capitals of columns, as well as the zodiacal figures on the ceiling, announce it was one of the principal temples of Egypt. The figures and hieroglyphs are somewhat larger than those of Dendera…"

On the 20th of August, Giovanni and Sarah arrived at Edfu.

"The propylean is the largest and most perfect of any in Egypt. It is covered on all sides with colossal figures of intaglio relevato, and contains several apartments in the interior, which receive light by square apertures in the side…. Farther still is a small temple, almost unnoticed by travelers, which has an avenue of sphinxes leading in a right line towards the great temple. The sphinxes, several of which I

Giovanni and Sarah traveling up the Nile through the Second Cataract (Nubia). 19th Century

cleared from the sand, have a lion's body and female head as large as life. There are vast heaps of ruins, all-round these temples, and many relics of antiquity may be buried there."

Giovanni left Edfu and on the 22nd of August and arrived at Kom Ombo (Ombos, Upper Egypt)." *The columns of the portico form one of the richest groups of architecture I have ever seen. The hieroglyphs are well executed and some still retain their colors."*

Giovanni and Sarah traveled deeper into Egypt, untouched and unchanged by the nineteenth century, and on the 27th arrived at the Island of Philae. *"My anxiety to see the ruins was as great as my expectations, but when I beheld them, they surpassed everything that imagination could anticipate. "*

As they approached the temple, Giovanni and Sarah were being watched by the local natives. *"A few natives came to watch us armed with spears and shields covered in crocodile skins. Their appearance was rather alarming and I thought it was time to be on our guard".* When the natives approached the boat, Giovanni armed with a pistol, pointed to the natives if they attack them or harm Sarah, they would pay the consequences. The natives dispersed, leaving Giovanni and Sarah to explore the temple

The ruins of Ombos. Sketched and painted by Belzoni

Temple of Edfu

Interior of the Temple of Philae. Sketched and painted by Giovanni Belzoni. 19t century

grounds. Venturing the temple compounds, Giovanni discovered an exquisite piece for the British Museum.

"I observed several blocks of stones, with hieroglyphics on them in great perfection, that might be taken away, and an obelisk of granite about twenty-two feet in length, and two in breadth. I think this also might be easily be

removed, as it lies in a good situation, and not far from the waterside."

On the 6th of September, Giovanni and Sarah, at last, arrived at the fabled *'castle in the Air'.*

"In front of the minor temple are six colossal figures, which make a better appearance at a distance than when near them. they are thirty feet high, and are hewn out of the rock, as is also the large temple, which has one figure of an enormous size, with the head and shoulders, only projecting out of the sand, and notwithstanding the great distance, I could perceive, that it was beautifully decorated....The sand from the north side, accumulated by the wind on the rock above the temple which had gradually descended towards its front choked the entrance and buried two-thirds of it.

Although the herculean figures sticking out from the sands amazed Giovanni, on approaching the figures

Lithograph of the Temple of Abu Simbel buried in an ocean of sands.

closely, Belzoni had a hard time finding the entrance. *"On my approaching this temple, the hope I had formed of opening its entrance vanished at once, for the amazing accumulation of sand was such, that it appeared an impossibility ever to reach the door."*

Despite the lack of an entrance, Belzoni believed the door was further up. *"We ascended a hill of sand at the upper part of the temple, and there found the head of a hawk projecting out of the sand*

Abul Simbel (1264-1244 BC)

Local legends had it the temple of Abu Simbel had gold inside it, but the temple was more than a depository of gold. At Abu Simbel, Ramses II had two herculean temples to be cut directly out of the hillside. Each statue, towering at 66ft, portrays Ramses II as he wears both the double crown of Upper and Lower Egypt, and the nemes headdress. Above the main entrance, rests the sun god Re-Horahkhty. The largest celebrated Ramses II as a mighty warrior Pharaoh and praising his greatest military feat.

The smaller temple, facing the east, was dedicated to Hathor, the cow-headed goddess of love, and Ramses II's great love and royal wife, Queen Nefertari. An inscription describes the love Ramses had for Nefertari. *'Ramses he has made a temple for Nefertari for whose very sake the sun does shine'*.Together, Ramses, Nefertari, and his lesser wives had many children ranging from 80 sons to 60 daughters; ensuring the Ramseide bloodline would continue for centuries to come. On the temples, the

The Herculean statues of Ramses II cut directly into the mountainside of Abu Simbel. 19th Dynasty

façades are two statues of Nefertari (33ft) and four statues of Ramses himself. Nefertari wears the double feathered cow horned and sun disc crown of Hathor. What made these statues special was Ramses presenting his wife to the world not only as a symbol of his love for his queen but as equal in stature and power. In 1255 BC, Ramses II and Nefertari travel to inaugurate the opening of the great temple. Today, Abu Simbel is still considered a wonder of the ancient world.

The smaller temple is dedicated to Queen Nefertari. 19th Dynasty

Sketch of Abu Simbel by Giovanni Belzoni. 19th Century

only to its neck. From the situation of this figure, I concluded it to be over the door." However, there was still the issue of all the sand covering the temple. *"The sand ran down in a slope from one side to the other, and to attempt to make an aperture straight through it to the door would have been like making a hole in the water."* At first glance, it seemed impossible to remove the excess amount of sands but, Belzoni believed there was a way to do it.

Seeing this as a new challenge, Giovanni set out to Dongola, a remote village "cut off" from the Pasha's domain to secure workers for his monumental task. Problems began for the extravagant adventurer when he couldn't procure the men needed for this monumental task. For starters, the fellahs of the area didn't understand the value of money. in their minds, why should they endure hard labor for pieces of useless metal?

The Dauod (the local leader) told Giovanni it was useless to convince them since another Frank, named Drovetti, had tried the same tactic and failed to rally the fellahs to work for him; however, Belzoni was undeterred. He politely informs the Dauod he would convince the fellahs to work for him but failed to do so when none showed up the next day. With no luck at Abu Simbel, Giovanni decided to explore the rest of Nubia. During this time, Giovanni met with the Cacheff, and after tight negotiating with the Cacheff,

The Temple of Abu Simbel and the smaller temple of Queen Nefertari on the banks of the Nile River.

it was agreed that if the temple contained any gold, Giovanni would give half to the Cacheff as a gift, but if there were no gold and only "rocks" Giovanni was permitted to take them.

The Cacheff also allowed Giovanni to make drawings as well. Upon returning to Abu Simbel Giovanni began the arduous task to remove the sands and to begin to unearth the herculean temple; however, things didn't go according to plans.

Lithograph of Abu Simbel and the smaller temple on the coastline of the Nile River

First, the fellahs failed to show up on the first day. After negotiating an equal pay, the fellahs showed up, but when they did work they barely worked and complained that removing the sands was too hard and exhausting. At the end of each day, Giovanni reluctantly had to pay these men doing half the work they were supposed to do.

Second, the provisions he was promised were either delayed or were outright not given to him unless he presents a gift to the Dauod as leverage; it didn't help the Daoud was having issues with his brother, who too was a leader of his village. At one point both brothers confronted each other and fought over the gifts Belzoni had brought. Lastly, Giovanni was running out of food and money. Due to these circumstances, Belzoni had no choice but to suspend his work at Abu Simbel after seven grueling days, but promised the Daoud if he will guard the site, he would return to finish what he started.

Chapter 7

Belzoni The Archaeologist

Having run out of money and provisions, Giovanni returned to the island of Philae to take possession of the topside obelisk standing in front of the temple of Isis as a gift for the British government; however, in his travels, Giovanni had collected various artifacts for the British Museum and there was no room left. Instead, Belzoni left it behind and took back with him "twelve pieces of stone" small enough to fit on the bloated boat. This obelisk, though not important as of now, would become a critical key in deciphering the hieroglyphics and unlocking Egypt's forgotten past.

On the 7th of October, Giovanni and Sarah returned to Thebes to see the Memnon and the lid of the sarcophagus still resting where they previously left it two months prior. After securing a boat to transport the Memnon and the lid to Alexandria, Belzoni decided to do some digging at Karnak. It was at Karnak where Giovanni made the first in a line of extraordinary discoveries such as the ram-headed sphinxes.

    Digging at Karnak's southern district, the Temple of Mut, Belzoni discovered eighteen preserved statues, yet out of the eighteen, only six were perfect. These six being five black granite statues of the lion-headed goddess Sekhmet and one giant white granite statue of Pharaoh Setlios II; however, when he wanted to excavate the entirety of the temple, he was a force to end his dig at Karnak. This was due to Drovetti's agents stirring the fellahs against Belzoni and not wanting to cause any trouble, ended his time at Karnak. As soon as he left, Drovetti and his agents took over the site.

    Belzoni bummed he could no longer dig at Karnak, decided to take up research in an area Drovetti wasn't digging at known as Beban el Malook (the famed Valley of the Kings). *"It was in the western*

Statue of the Lion-headed goddess Sekhmet. Rosicrucian Museum, San Jose, CA.

Procession of Ram headed Sphinxes located at Karnak, Thebes

valley that one of the French savants discovered a large tomb, which he found open, but was quite unknown before his time. I went to visit this tomb, and found it very extensive, and in pretty good preservation." As he was exploring the area, Belzoni came across stones that appeared to be converging around something.

He took a long stick and pushed it into the stones. As the stick continued to go deeper into the rock bed, Belzoni discovered it went deeper than should. This meant there was something underneath the rocks; perhaps even an intact tomb. Before he could procure men to test his hypothesis, both he and Sarah were struck with an intense case of ophthalmia. Common in the time of Belzoni, ophthalmia was an inflammation of the eyes.

Since Giovanni wasn't a native of Egypt, he didn't have resistance to the unrelenting sun; thus rendering Belzoni effectively blind. Though this blindness was temporary but left him bedridden for three weeks. When Belzoni recovered, he took some fellahs and returned to the spot he left three weeks prior and began removing the stones. It would take Belzoni and the fellahs just two hours to unearth the entrance to the tomb.

> *"I cannot boast of having made a great discovery in this tomb, though it contains several curious and singular painted figures on the walls, and from extent, and part of a sarcophagus remaining in the center of a large chamber, have reason to suppose, that it was the burial-place of some person of distinction".*

Sekhmet

Amongst the lengthy pantheon of Egyptian deities, the lion-headed goddess Sekhmet was the most feared and dangerous god amongst the Egyptians. The name Sekhmet means *'she who is powerful'*. Known as the *'eye of Ra'* Sekhmet represented the destructive aspect of the sun god Ra. According to Egyptian mythology, Ra tasked Sekhmet to punish his creation, mortals, for rebelling against his will, but when Sekhmet got a taste of mortal blood, she began to eradicate the mortals. Sekhmet lost so much control she nearly wiped out all of humanity. Seeing his daughter destroying his creation, Ra asked the other gods to trick Sekhmet into drinking large quantities of beer laced in blood. Sekhmet fell for the trick and drank until she fell asleep. Due to their deception, Sekhmet angrily left Egypt, but her absence caused the diminishing of the sun's power and nearly ended the world. It was only the god Thoth who convinced her to come back. In depictions, Sekhmet is depicted wearing the sun disc representing her connection with Ra.

Sarcophagus of Pharaoh Ay. From WV23, 18th Dynasty

The tomb Giovanni discovered belonged to the Pharaoh Aye, uncle to the boy king Tutankhamun. This tomb is referred to as WV23 but would be later dubbed as the *'tomb of the 12 Monkeys'*. On the tomb's entrance, Giovanni carved his name: *DISCOVERED BY BELZONI-1816.*

Back at Thebes, Belzoni was eager to transport all his discoveries for the British Museum; however, the Camikan issued another edict. This new edict prohibited the transportation of stones along the Nile; another ploy by Drovetti to hinder Belzoni from succeeding any further. To make matters worse for

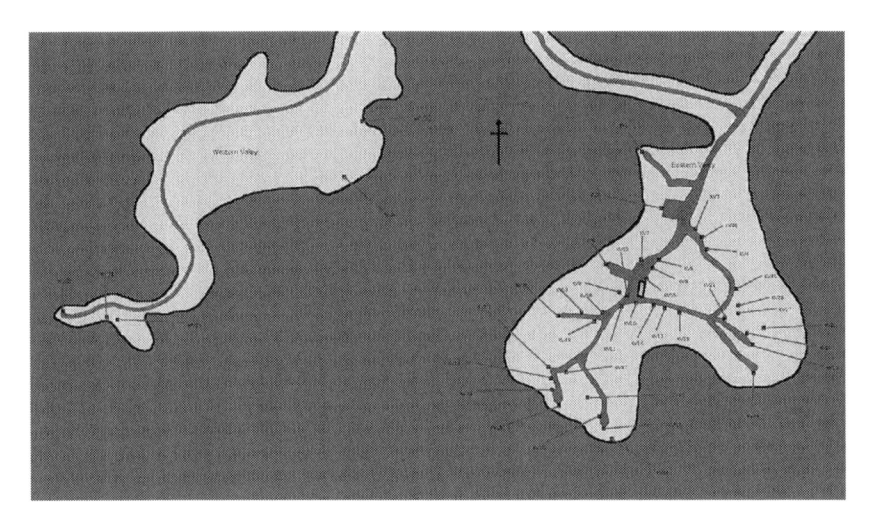

The layout of the Valley of the Kings with each marker representing every tomb discovered since the Nineteenth Century

Modern Day Valley of the Kings

Belzoni, the boatmen he hired to transport the colossi bust outright refused. They feared that due to the bust's weight, would cause the boat to cave in on itself. Turns out this was, again, a ploy by Drovetti who ordered his agents to threaten the boatmen to hinder his competition progress. To solve this problem, Giovanni met with Khali Bey (son-in-law of Muhamad Ali who married the Pashas daughter Nazil) who was the governor of Upper Egypt. After the exchange of gifts dining, and civil negotiations with the boatmen, the problem was solved, and Giovanni was allowed to transport his collection.

For the next five days, Giovanni's collection was loaded safely onboard and on the 20th of November 1816, the Younger Memnon set sailed for Cairo. Belzoni and Sarah set off the following day; however, the next twenty-four-day trip would prove to be terrible for the Paduan. He was once again struck with ophthalmia and had to endure twelve grueling days alone locked in his cabin so his eyes could heal.

On the 15th of December, Belzoni and Sarah arrived in Cairo. After dropping off Sarah at their home with James waiting, Giovanni headed to the British Consul to meet with Mr. Salt, but when he got there, he was met with Salt's secretary, Mr. Beechey (William Henry Beechey). Beechey, informs Belzoni he just missed Salt and was currently at Alexandria, but before he left, he instructed Belzoni that any artifacts he collected on his journey were to be stored at the consulate. Perplexed, Belzoni argued that everything he unearthed should go to the British

Portrait of Sir William Henry Beechey, circa 1800. Like Belzoni, he too was an artist who would go on to help the Paduan paint and record ancient monuments

Museum; however, it was explicit that only the head was going to the British Museum. These instructions raised red flags for Giovanni but decided to brush it off for the time being; believing his collection would eventually be taken to the British Museum

Giovanni, traveling alongside the colossi bust, arrived at Alexandria in early January 1817. He hoped his collection would build him a reputation in England and wanted to encourage his patron, Mr. Salt, to go south to Nubia again. He met with Mr. Salt to discuss his plan for a second trip into Upper Egypt and Nubia and opening the temple at Abu Simbel.

At first, Belzoni thought Salt would say no, but what he got was the exact opposite. Due to the accomplishment Belzoni displayed with moving the Younger Memnon, Mr. Salt was more than happy to accept his proposal; however, he didn't have the necessary funds to fund an expedition to Abu Simbel but would fund any dig he deemed worthy of excavation. Dismayed he wouldn't be able to return to Abu Simbel sooner than he thought, Belzoni was still delighted by this revelation.

He asked Salt for artists to accompany him to Abu Simbel and record it; however, Salt instead offered Mr. Beechey, who was an exquisite painter, to accompany him. With his proposal accepted, Belzoni left to prepare for his next trip. As for Sarah, Giovanni reluctantly decided to leave her in the care of Mr. Cochini, the British chancellor who had a residence in Egypt, and his family. Giovanni still felt Nubia was too dangerous for Sarah after an incident at Abu Simbel when their boat was surrounded by fellahs causing Sarah to brandish her pistol to them. On the 20th of February 1817, Belzoni, Mr. Beechey, and Greek excavator Giovanni d'Athanasi (Salt's agent) and set off to Boolak.

Chapter 8
The Next Adventure

On their way to Boolak, Giovanni and his crew were able to get a great view of the Great Pyramids the Step Pyramid; however, they were forced to make a stop at the Tabeen village and wait out the winds. During their stop, they came across a Bedouin encampment. The Bedouins were quite friendly to Belzoni and his crew and told him about a statue half-buried in the sands at the village of Boorumbol. Excited for obtaining an exquisite piece this early, Giovanni traveled to the Boorumbol only to discover there was no statue. *"On our arrival, we were shown a piece of rock, which had not the form of anything."* Though bummed, Belzoni found this as a harmless joke and returned to his boat and resumed his travel to Boolak. As they settled in the village of Meimond, Belzoni and his crew happened to stumble upon an

Lithograph of a Bedouin encampment. Drawn and painted by Giovanni Belzoni

Arabic festival going on:

The performers consisted of about thirty men, all in a row, clapping their hands in concert, so as to form a kind of accompaniment to their song, which consisted of three or four words, and with one foot before the other keeping a sort of perpetual motion, but without changing their hands. Before the men were two women with daggers in their hands, also in continual action, running toward the men and then returning from them with an extraordinary motion, brandishing their daggers and waving their garments….This is a sort of Bedouin dance, and is the most decent of all that I ever saw."

Having spectators watch their dance in motion, the Bedouin women decided to give an encore for Belzoni and his crew and danced throughout the night.

    The following morning, Belzoni and crew headed towards the town of Minieh where Giovanni met with a fellow European named Mr. Brine. Brine, who introduced sugar baking into Egypt, invited Belzoni and crew to his home for refreshments. As they discussed, Mr. Brine informs Belzoni that Drovetti was making a forced march to Thebes. Drovetti hoped that by being the first one there would grant him access to not only the site but to all the artifacts the fellahs had dug the previous year.

    Giovanni was worried the collection he hid, the sphinxes and Sekhmet's, were in danger of being taken by Drovetti."*I had no doubt if they reached*

Lithograph of Arabic dancing. Drawn and painted by Giovanni Belzoni

Thebes before us, they would take possession of that ground, and we should have no longer a right to explore it." To get to Thebes faster, Belzoni decided to travel not on the Nile, but donkeys.

He believed traveling on land was the fastest way to travel and could cover more distance than by boat. *"I was not long therefore considering the matter, and resolved to set off immediately, and by traveling day and night was in hopes to reach the place before them."* To accompany him on this arduous journey was Athanasi while Beechey traveled by boat. This would give Drovtetti the illusion he was traveling on boat and not on land. Once securing their provisions, Giovanni and Athanasi set off into the night.

> *"By this time it was midnight, yet we set off immediately, and forced marches brought us on the next morning to Manfalout. From this place we hastened without delay, and arrived at Siout before daylight. At sunrise we mounted again and arrived at dark at Tahta. Here we rested in the convent for hours started afresh by the light of the moon, and arrived at Girgeh in the night…..The whole of our journey occupied five days and a half, during which I slept eleven hours…*

When they arrived at Thebes, Belzoni believed he had beaten Drovetti, but that was not the case.

Lithograph of the ruins of the hypostyle Karnak temple (Thebes). Drawn and painted by Giovanni Belzoni

Belzoni saw a French flag fluttering in the hot winds and knew he was too late: Drovetti had beaten him. He saw Fellahs dropping off fine pieces of antiquity into a growing pile. Drovetti's agents had arrived before Belzoni and bribed the Cacheff with extravagant gifts and in doing so, obtained permission to excavate Karnak; including the spot where Belzoni dug the previous year.

Forced to spectate Drovetti's crew digging up ancient artifacts, Belzoni decided to find somewhere else to dig that Drovetti didn't have claim over. He decided to explore the ancient necropolis of Gouraou. As he explored *"the burial-place of the great city of a hundred gates,"* Belzoni came across the stench of mummies and large amounts of choking dust.

> *"A vast quantity of dust rises, so fine that it enters into the throat and nostrils, and chokes the nose and mouth to such a degree, that it requires great power of lungs to resist it and the strong effluvia of the mummies...But what a rest! Surrounded*

Mummification

One of Egypt's defining legacies is the numerous mummies discovered throughout the country, but why did the Egyptians mummify their dead? In ancient times, the Egyptians believed in the concept of duality. The plain where they stood was a secondary Egypt created by the gods to mirror their own, but much better, Egypt. Every Egyptian lived their life in preparing for the next life; in which they believed they were going to a better Egypt. Their whole culture was preparing for the afterlife.

The process of mummification was all about preserving the spirit for the next stage. The Egyptians developed and refined the process over the centuries; resulting in some of the best-preserved mummies in history. Once the deceased has passed, the body was taken to a special place known as the Red Land; a desert region far from Egypt's heavily populated towns but had access to the Nile.

The priests would place the body at Ibu or the *'Place of Purification* where the body was thoroughly washed and cleaned with palm wine and water from

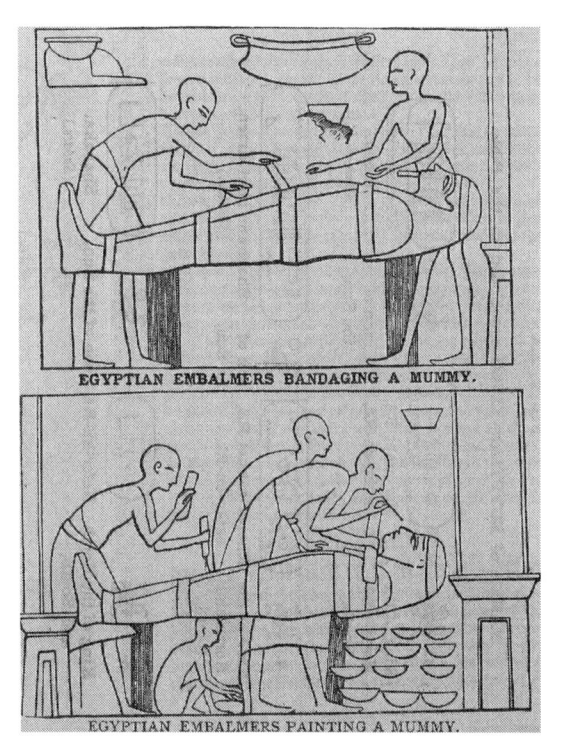

Priests removing the organs and brain of the deceased

the Nile. After the body was cleansed and purified, it was taken to *per nefer* or *'house of mummification'* to begin the lengthy and gruesome removal of the internal organs. The men working on the body were experts in anatomy and knew the human body inside and out. A small incision was made to the left side of the abdomen where the lungs, intestines, liver, and stomach were removed. From there, they were washed with water and covered in natron (salt), and packed into canopic jars.

The only organ the Egyptians refused to remove was the heart. They believed the heart was the home to intelligence and the individual's being. The one organ the Egyptians believed was useless was the brain. A long hook ended rod was inserted through the nostril where it punctured the skull as it violently broke stirred the brain until it was drained out of the individual's nose!

Their body was once more cleansed with water and covered in oils to keep the skin from decaying as they stuffed the body with salt bags as dummies for the once internal organs. Then, the body was placed in a natron bath for forty days for the natron to absorb all water within the body and dry it out. In the final stages, the most skilled wore a jackal mask representing the god of the dead and mummification Anubis. This, symbolized Anubis being the one overseeing the mummification of the individual. The body is first wrapped from head to

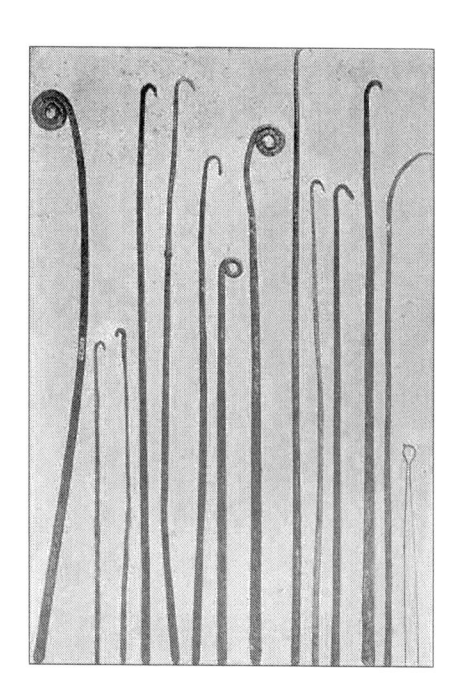

Medical tools used for the mummification process. These were the metal hooks used to remove the brain as it was deemed useless

neck, fingers, and toes, as the arms and legs are the last to be wrapped. Special amulets were placed within the bandages to protect the deceased as it journeys the afterlife; as priests preside over the body with prayers of protection against evil spirits. All of this was done for the *ba* (the soul) and the *ka* (life force) to come together to be reborn in the next life.

Surrounded by bodies, heaps of mummies in all directions, which, previous to be accustomed to the sight impressed me with horror."

In the dark filled cave, Belzoni began exploring the catacombs to find papyri worth taking for the British Museum; however, Belzoni started to get lightheaded from breathing in so much dust.

      Giovanni felt as if he was being choked and decided to sit down to catch his breath. *"...Nearly overcome, I sought a resting place, found one, and contrived to sit, but when my weight bore on the body of an Egyptian, it crushed it like a bandbox."* Stunned by what was happening, Belzoni tried to course-correct and not further damage the mummy, but it was too late!

"I naturally had recourse to my hands to sustain my weight, but they found no better support so that I sunk altogether among the broken mummies,

Papyri of the Nun, god of water and chaos, lifting the barque
(boat) of Ra represented as the scarab beetle into the sky

with a crash of bones, rags, and wooden cases, which
raised such a dust as kept me motionless for a
quarter of an hour...and every step I took I crushed
a mummy in some part or other."

Though modern archaeologists view this moment as Belzoni desecrating mummies and artifacts by stepping on them, we need to remember archaeology and Egyptology was still in its infancy; with Belzoni's action acting more as an accident than intentional.

As he traversed the dust invested catacombs, Belzoni discovered papyri-covered in the same cloth as the mummies- hidden under the chest and arms of the mummies and tucked them into his bag. On his return from the necropolis, Belzoni met a local Fellah who presented to him a bronze vase coated in hieroglyphics.

Taking a liking to the vase, Belzoni purchased the vase from the Fellah. Luckily for Giovanni, it wasn't a fake and still resides today at the British Museum. Belzoni returned to Beban-el-Malook to see if there were any further discoveries to be made. One day, Belzoni discovered a small opening to a tomb. to open the tomb, Belzoni used a "large sludge-hammer" to create a large hole to enter the tomb. Once the hole was large enough, Belzoni entered the

Sarcophagus of Ramses III. 19th Dynasty

tomb and discovered a small chamber- though the tomb had sharp projecting rocks emanating from the ceiling- with a granite sarcophagus belonging to Ramses III, son of Ramses II, with its lid perfectly intact. Amongst the numerous mummies, Belzoni found more papyri.

After Drovetti concluded his excavations at Karnak, Belzoni was finally allowed to dig at the Temple Mut. Choosing a new location to dig, Belzoni discovered four new perfectly preserved statues of Sekhmet. It was also at Thebes where Belzoni uncovered the large red granite colossi of Pharaoh Thutmose III; missing only one arm but found it not too far from the statue. *"It was of red granite, of beautiful workmanship and uncommonly well preserved, except one ear, and part of the chin, which had been knocked off along the beard"*.

But Belzoni wasn't done at Karnak. At the Temple of Montu, Belzoni removed the *"famous altar with the six divinities"* and placed it amongst his other discoveries i.e. the four Sekhmet's and the lid of Ramses III. Around this time, Belzoni met Count de

Forbin, the director of the Louvre Museum who he sold four intact statues of Sekhmet. Why would Giovanni sell off his pieces to the French knowing they were his rivals? Drovetti's doctor, Doctor Moroki, was the head excavator at Thebes and uncovered his collection and claimed it as their own, but Forbin claimed a man had dug it before them; that being Belzoni himself. In gratitude, Belzoni sold them to Forbin where they still reside to change; however, this new friendship wouldn't last.

    It seemed fortune favored Belzoni; however, that was about to change. For quite some time, Drovetti's agents had continued spying on Belzoni's continual success and this enraged the Italian. It seemed wherever Belzoni dug, he finds artifacts better than Drovetti. To get back at Belzoni, Drovetti pressured the Defterdar Bey to issue a decree.

> "It is the will and pleasure of Hamed, the Defterder By and present ruler of Upper Egypt, that no Sheiks, Fellahs, or other persons, shall from this moment sell any article of antiquity to the

Animal Mummies

During his time at Gournou, Giovanni uncovered forgotten mummies; however, he uncovered the mummified remains of animals. *"I must not omit, that among these tombs we saw some which contained the mummies of animals intermixed with human bodies. There were bulls, cows, sheep, monkeys, foxes, bats, crocodiles, fishes, and birds, in them: idols often occur, and one tomb was filled with nothing but cats, carefully folded in red and white linen, the head covered by a mask representing the cat, and made of the same linen. I have opened all these sorts of animals. Of the bull, the calf, and the sheep, there is no part, but the head which is covered with linen, and the horns projecting out of the cloth, the rest of the body being represented by two pieces of wood, eighteen inches wide and three feet long, in a horizontal direction, at the end of which was another, placed perpendicularly, two feet high, to form the breast of the animal."*

In Ancient Egypt, the Egyptians had a symbiotic relationship with their gods and goddesses. They believed the gods and goddesses dwelled amongst their creation in the guise of animals. For instance, the god of knowledge Thoth could take the form of the ibis or baboon; the god of the Nile. Sobek in the guise of a crocodile or the beloved Bastet who takes the form of a cat.

    These animals were treated as if they were the gods themselves and when they died, they too were mummified. Despite there being vast quantities of animal mummies today, not all are perfectly preserved. Their bones or tiny fragments are what's left of the animals. Originally, it was believed these animal mummies were wild animals; however, a new study showed these animals were bred and taken care of by their handlers before mummification.

Lithograph of animal mummies and arches. Drawn and painted by Giovanni Belzoni

English party, or work for them, on the contrary, it is hereby ordered, that everything that may be found shall be sold to the party of Mr. Drovetti, and whoever disobeys this order will incur the displeasure of the Bey."

As you can expect, Belzoni didn't take this mandate kindly, but had no choice and had to end his operations at Karnak and Thebes again.

With Karnak closed off, Belzoni decided to return to the island of Philae. Before he left, Giovanni sent a letter to Mr. Salt. *"I had suggested to Mr. Salt that, if he could send us a supply of money, we would proceed to open the temple of Abu Simbel, a project that was deemed nearly imaginary, a castle in the air, as no one supposed any temple really existed there."*

Once securing his collection from Drovetti's agents in an artificial mud wall Belzoni, Mr. Beechey, and Athanasi set off for the island of Philae. on the 23rd of May 1817. After eleven days on the Nile, Giovanni and his crew landed on the island of Philae.

During their time at Philae, Giovanni stopped to check up on his collection to see if they were unharmed or destroyed by Drovetti's men, but luckily for the showman, the obelisk was still top sided and his collection untouched. From there, he decided to observe the ruins in more detail:

> *"The style of the hieroglyphics proves, that the edifice on it is of the last era of the Egyptian nation: in my opinion, of the time of the Ptolemies….The whole ruins consist of two temples nearly united together. The small temple, dedicated, I believe, to the same goddess, to Serapis, and to the rest of the gods….*
>
> *At the entrance of the first portal lies the obelisk of granite, thrown down, as mentioned before, its pedestal having a Greek inscription on it, which is complaint of the priests, addressed to Ptolemy and*

Print of Giovanni Belzoni adopting Arabic garb and a long beard.

Cleopatra….The inscription was discovered by an English traveler, Mr. Banks, who, not having time to dig it out, left it, and Mr. Beechey took a copy of it."

These moments of observations demonstrate Giovanni acting more than just a raider, but as a scholar. Belzoni went as far as creating a wax sculpture of the great temple, but due to the heat excessing over 124 degrees melted.

    One day, as Giovanni and his crew rested in the temple, a Fellah arrived on the island with a letter from Mr. Salt. *"The letter brought us a supply of money, and, to my great satisfaction, Mr. Salt complied with my wishes of opening the temple of Abu Simbel, which I had often suggested to him, and I must give him credit for risking the expense of such an undertaking…."* Now with the proper funding needed, Giovanni can fulfill his dream and uncover the secrets beneath the sands of the temple of Abu Simbel

Chapter 9

Opening the Temple of the Sands

Before Belzoni and co. embarked on Abu Simbel, he scooped up two new companions. These new companions were British naval captains James Mangles and Charles Leonard Irby. Mangles and Irby were on a tour of Egypt after the conclusion of the Napoleonic Wars (1804-1815) and had arrived at Philae on the 4th of June, few days before Belzoni received the letter for Mr. Salt. They were commemorating the king, George III's birthday through a salute of twenty-one guns (firing guns exactly twenty-one times) which scared the natives away!

After retelling his story of the great temple at Abu Simbel to the naval officers, both Mangles and Irby were intrigued by the prospects of discovering

Irby lithograph drawing of Philae (1823)

gold within the temple. They decided to join Belzoni and help open the temple.

On the 16th of June, Giovanni, Mr. Beechey, Mangles, Irby, and Athanasi left the island of Philae and headed straight to Abu Simbel. Once landing safely at Abu Simbel thirteen days later on the 29th, Belzoni picked up where he last left off the previous year but needed to renegotiate with the Cacehff for workers. *'At length, with much ado, I made a bargain for two piastres, to open that for him...'* Belzoni agreed to pay the workers three hundred piastres, and this time around, he got the workers he needed with no problems or excuses.

For the next three days, Belzoni, his crew, and eighty Fellahs laboriously removed the sand from the temple; however, on the third day, the Fellahs got tired of removing endless sands and left Giovanni and his crew to themselves. It also didn't help the next day being the first day of Ramadan and as a result, could not work but only feast and obey the holy law. It was now up to Belzoni and his crew (totaling in six) to open the temple.

Every morning, Belzoni and his ragtag crew rose early to remove the sands choking the temple and left two hours after sunrise, yet the summer season was against them. The crew grew tired of removing the sands under the unforgiving heat and stopped working. *"Three weeks we labored on the dune, that time of the year the heat was intense, and digging in the sand was like making a hole in water."* Even Belzoni, who was the last man standing, too

Façade of Abu Simbel

grew tired of the heat and digging and gave up as well.

Though stopped by the endless sands, Belzoni was determined to find the solution to this problem and he soon found it: water. By drawing water from the Nile, Belzoni and his crew would pour it over sands and dampen the sand. This method made an incredible impression on the dune. Now driven by the prospect of unearthing the entrance to the temple, Giovanni and co. worked endlessly for another three weeks. At last, on the 1st of August 1817, Belzoni found the opening to the temple. In the early morning, Belzoni and his crew entered the temple. Belzoni had become the first person in over three thousand years to set foot in the temple. Upon entering the temple, Belzoni was in awe of what was to be held.

> *"From what we can perceive at the first view, it was evidently a very large place, but our astonishment increased, when we found it to be one of the most magnificent of temples enriched*

Sideview of the exterior of Abu Simbel

Interior of Abu Simbel; the herculean standing statues of Ramses II

with beautiful intaglios, painting, colossal figures, etc."

Belzoni was astounded by the large colonnade of colossi figures of the then-unknown Ramses II.

> *" We entered at first into a large pronaos, fifty-seven feet long and fifty-two wide, supported by two rows of square pillars in a line from the front door to the door of the sekos....The tops of their turbans reach the ceiling, which is about thirty feet high."*

As he traversed the temple, Belzoni came across benches to sit, vast wall reliefs coated in hieroglyphics, and scenes depicting Ramses II defeating his enemies, the Hittites, at the Battle of Kadesh.

At the end of the temple, Belzoni came across a little shrine. *"The sanctuary is twenty-three feet and*

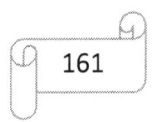

Battle of Kadesh

During the reign of Seti I, Egypt had maintained their influence over the Phoenician coast; while the Hittites, the new power of Western Anatolia (modern-day Turkey) controlled territory north of Kadesh. Kadesh was more of a fortress that had access to northern trading routes. Seti I had captured the city of Kadesh from the Hittites years prior, but as soon as he left, the people- who sworn their allegiance to Egypt- turned right around and allied themselves with the Hittites; resulting in Kadesh being reclaimed without a fight.

In Year 4 of Ramses II's reign, he vowed to stamp his might and authority on Egypt's eastern vassals by reclaiming the fortress city of Kadesh. After a revolt broke out in the Levant, Ramses II led his troops across the Sini land bridge and reasserted Egypt's claims over the Phoenician ports and Canaan. In Year 5, Ramses II decided it was time to recapture Kadesh. He conscripted 20,000 soldiers, the greatest army Egypt had ever seen and rode east to the city. Ramses' large army was divided into four divisions-

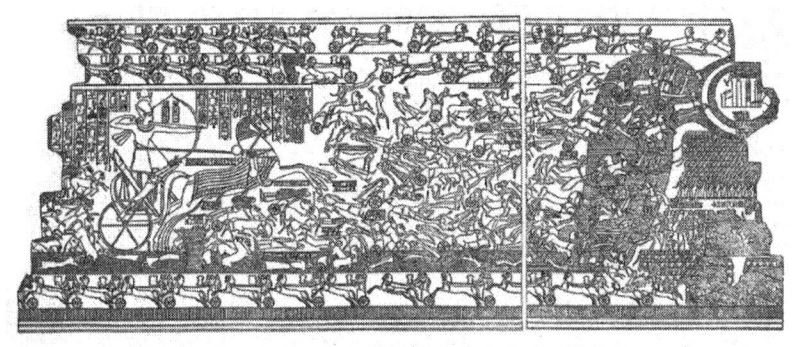

BATTLE SCENE FROM THE GREAT KADESH RELIEFS OF RAMSES II ON THE WALLS OF THE RAMESSEUM.

Wall relief depicting the Battle of Kadesh at Abu Simbel

with 5,000 men in each division- protected by a specific god: Ptah (Memphis) Seth (Avaris or the Northern Delta), Amun (Thebes), and Ra (Heliopolis). Ramses, at the head of the army, made his way through Canaan, south of Syria, and made it to the Bekaa Valley in early May.

As he was preparing to cross the River Orontes to Kadesh, Rameses guards discovered two Hittite deserters stalking the camps. They relayed to Ramses their king, Muwatallis, was too scared to fight the mighty king and was cowering one hundred miles away from Kadesh. Unbeknownst to Ramses, these two deserters were spies. Overconfident with this information, Ramses marched on ahead to Kadesh leading the Amun division, but before he moved forward, he had Ra division to follow closely behind and left Ptah and Seth on the other side of the Orontes.

Ramses planned to unite all his forces to conquer the city; however, Ramses got a rude awakening. Ramses guards captured two new spies who told a different story: Muwatalis wasn't cowering 100 miles from the city, but was already at the city waiting to strike. Ramses frantically had his family- Ramses brought his family to witness his quick victory- safely taken out of the camps and ordered his war council to send word to the remaining divisions to come to his aid, but it was too late.

The Hittites attacked. Muwatalis' force, twice the size of Ramses' forces, descended onto the camp. Ramses knew he was in the battle of his life. But what came next, according to the inscriptions at Ybsambul, was the stuff of legend. Ramses proclaimed at that moment, had a vision of his divine power. *"I was like fire! I was like a falcon pouncing! I was like a lion with its prey. I alone against millions of foreign enemies was triumphant! I killed and killed until they laid thrown together in their blood!*

Ramses singlehandedly defeated the entirety of the Hittite army; however, that could not be further from the truth. What happened was Ramses was outnumbered and was about to lose until Muwatalis made a grave error. He didn't commit his infantry to ambush Ramses and Ra division, which resulted in Ramses being saved at the last minute by his arriving forces from the east. Startled, Muwatalis and his men retreated across the Orontes.

The next day, Ramses and Muwatlis negotiated peace and left Kadesh. On his return to Egypt, knowing he had lost, Ramses decided to turn his defeat at Kadesh into a victory. He ordered every monument, relief, and temple walls plastered with his victory at Kadesh. He even went as far as having poetry written about Kadesh. The people unknowingly fell for Ramses showmanship but was all a farce since Ramses knew he had lost the battle and had to force peace with his enemy in humiliation. Egypt would never again fight a major war against a superpower.

Ramses II at the Battle of Kadesh. Painted by Carl Oderich (1865-1915)

Ramses II (on his chariot) smiting the Hittites. Wall relief from the Temple of Abu Simbel. 19th Dynasty

a half long, and twelve feet wide. It contains a pedestal in the center and at the end four colossal sitting figures, the heads of which are in good preservation, not having been injured by violence."

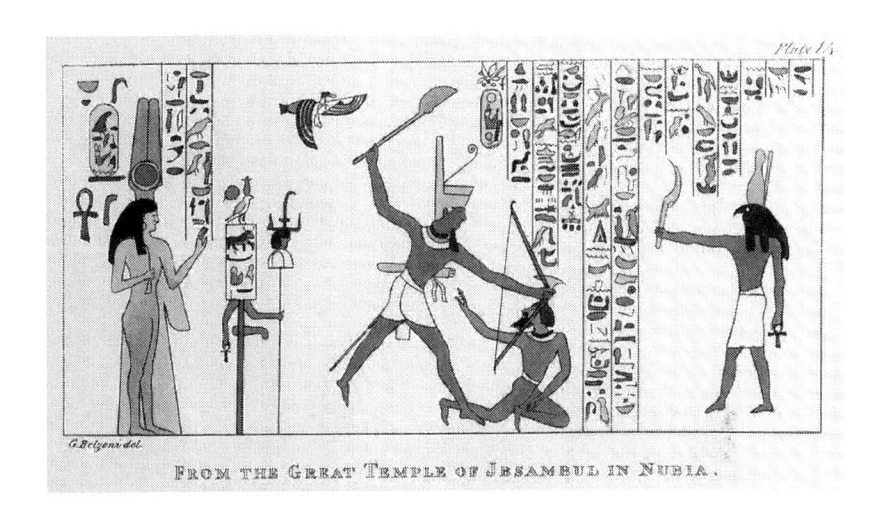

Ramses II smiting the Hittites, 19th Dynasty. Drawn and painted by Giovanni Belzoni.

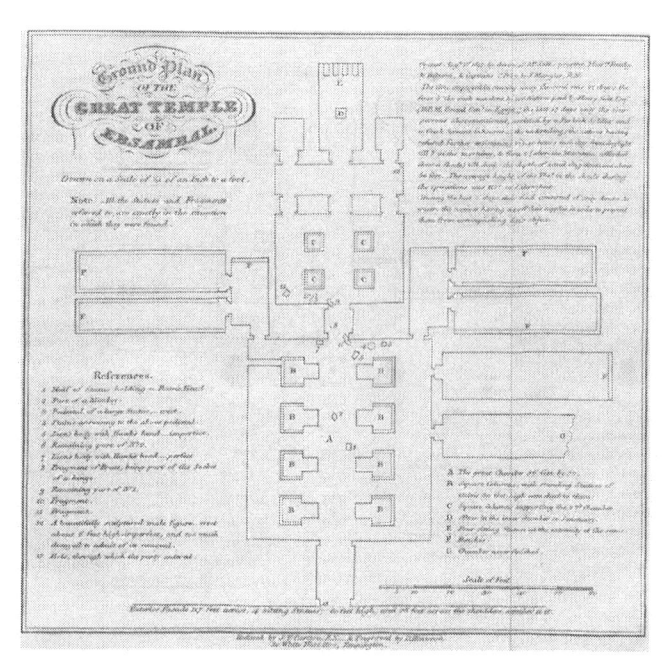

Interior layout of Ybsambul by Charles Irby.

Lithograph interior of Ybsambul. Drawn and painted by Giovanni Belzoni.

Painted recreation of how Abu Simbel was presented during the reign of Ramses II

(from left to right) Ptah, Amun, Ramses II, and Re-Horakhiti

These four figures within the small shrines were the gods Re-Horakhti, Amun-Re, Ptah- hidden in the shadows- and Ramses II. The Great Temple of Abu Simbel was a dedication to the life of the deified Ramses II. Despite unearthing the magnificent temple, the crew was disappointed in not finding any treasures, but not for Belzoni. He felt whoever this man was who built the temple was a real showman

(top) Architecture layout of Abu Simbel. (bottom) the herculean statues of Ramses II

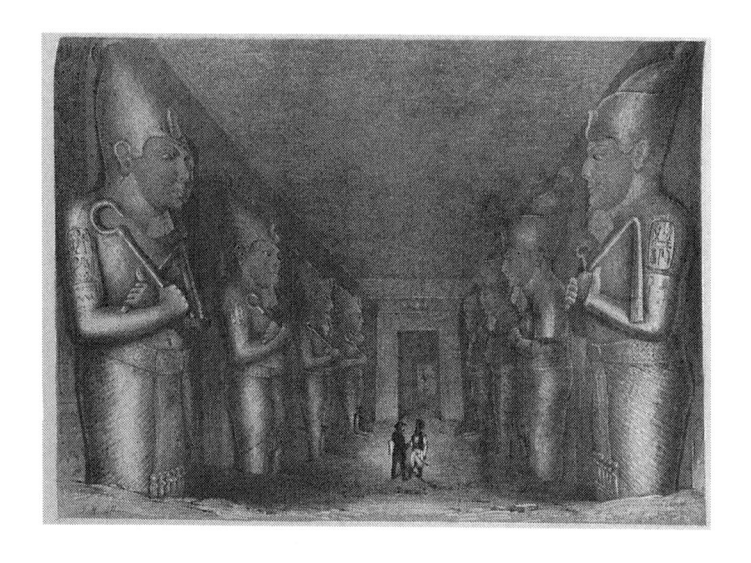

and what they discovered was more than enough.

Both Mangles and Irby compiled an inventory of what they found in the temple (two lions with "hawk's heads," copper tools, and a small sitting statue) while Belzoni and Mr. Beechey made drawings and outlines of the temple's interiors; especially the four seated statues. Twice a year, the rising sun illuminating three of the four statues with only Ptah, god of the underworld, shrouded in darkness. Even though it was morning, the temple had risen one hundred thirty degrees and Belzoni reaffirms how hot the temple was. *"The heat was so great in the interior of the temple, that it scarcely permitted us to take any drawings, as the perspiration from out hands soon rendered the paper quite wet."* To close out this adventure at Abu Simbel, Belzoni had his name and crew carve their names and date on the northern wall of the temple's sanctuary. No one, not even Drovetti, or Mr. Salt, was going to take away his accomplishment at Abu Simbel. On the 4th of August, Belzoni left Abu Simbel for the final time and embarked back to Luxor.

Chapter 10

Return to the Valley of The Kings

    After the remarkable discovery at Abu Simbel, Belzoni desired to discover and uncover more of Egypt's mysteries. He now wanted to introduce the world to this extraordinary ancient culture of Egypt. Giovanni felt comfortable with his connections to Great Britain and the British Museum, but now he wanted to go even further: to become the first scholar of Ancient Egypt in the world, but there was one problem. Belzoni wanted to continue his research at Thebes where it represented the best source of unearthing artifacts. Unfortunately for Giovanni, Drovetti still had a claim over digging sites at Thebes.

    Upon returning to Luxor, Mangles and Irby decided to head for Cairo but thanked Belzoni for an amazing adventure. As he disembarked from the boat, Giovanni was reunited with Sarah and James. While at Luxor, Belzoni heard a word of Drovetti's agents were now at Gournou overseeing digging sites from all directions and uncovered numerous mummies. Since Gournou was preoccupied with Drovetti, Belzoni made the smart decision and returned to the Valley of the Kings to pick up where he last left off on his research the previous year.

Upon entering the valley, Belzoni chose to explore the valley's western end where he first discovered the tomb of the '12 *Monkeys*' the previous year. It was during his extensive observation, Belzoni discovered what appeared to be an entrance to a tomb.

> *"Accordingly, I set the men to work near a hundred yards from the tomb which I discovered the year before, and when they had got a little below the surface, they came to some large stones, which had evidently been put there by those who closed the tomb."*

The workers began removing the large stones until an outline of a passage to the tomb was discovered; however, due to the intense heat, lead to exhaustion of the workers and Belzoni.

Giovanni decided to give everyone the rest of the day off and return the following morning. The next day, Belzoni returned intending to open the tomb through unconventional methods deemed amongst modern archaeologists as destructive and unorthodox.

> "I made a machine, not unlike a battering-ram. The walls resisted the blows of the Arabs for some time…but they contrived to make a breach at last, and in the same way, the opening was enlarged."

Belzoni immediately entered the tomb and as he descended the tomb steps, came across four intact mummies; as if they were just buried yesterday. As he explored the dank tomb, Giovanni came across

Sketch of a Medieval battering ram. Though not the same one used by Belzoni, the battering ram did its job at taking down impenetrable walls

four mummies in the same position as the other four. He observed how some of the mummies had a dual set of wrappings than the mummies he had uncovered up at this point. Belzoni deduced not every mummy was wrapped the same way and pointed out how these mummies were re-wrapped twice. Giovanni concluded these mummies in the

(top) Prince Mentuherkhepshef. Wall relief from KV19.
(bottom) Wall reliefs of KV19

tomb had to be either wealthy or members of the royal family.

Belzoni even went as far us unwrapping the mummies and found one had garlands of flowers and leaves, and on their heart, a metal plate with the image of Isis; however, Belzoni didn't find any gold or papyri though he was content with what he discovered. The decorated tomb Belzoni discovered belonged to Prince Mentuherkhepshef, who was the son of Pharaoh Ramses IX.

Despite finding a second tomb within the valley containing mummies, Giovanni believed deeply there was a tomb of an undiscovered king lying in wait to be unearthed. On the 6th of October 1817, Belzoni began new excavation south-east of the valley and on the 9th discovered a new tomb.

> " Though it is not extensive, they plastered it very finely with white, and painted some very fine figures on it in the most finished style....From the appearance, as it stands, it is plain, that they

intended to proceed, and that some particular event caused the work to be stopped. The painted figures on the wall are so perfect, that they are the best adapted of any I ever saw to give a correct and dear idea of the Egyptian taste."

Fortune seemed to favor Belzoni since on the same day he discovered this tomb, he discovered a secondary tomb. *"This is more extensive but entirely new, and without a single painting in it."*

Though eager to explore the tomb, Belzoni had to postpone his excavation. An English couple happened to be visiting Egypt and heard a word about Giovanni's discoveries at Luxor and the Valley of the Kings and wanted to meet the giant. Though a minor setback, Giovanni didn't mind spending the day showing them his discoveries; since it allowed him to flex his scholarly muscles.

Belzoni resumed his excavation on the 11th of October and discovered a secondary chamber. *"We found a sarcophagus of granite, with two mummies in it, and in a corner, a statue standing erect, six feet six inches high, and beautifully decorated cut out of sycamore-wood, it is nearly perfect except the nose."* Amongst the sarcophagus, the tomb was littered with figurines of animals.

> *"We found also a number of figures. Some had a lion's head, others, a fox's, others a monkey's. One had a land-tortoise instead of a head....In the chamber on our right hand we found another statue like the first, but not perfect. No doubt the had been placed on one side of the sarcophagus, holding a lamp or some offering in their hands, one hand being stretched out in the proper posture for this, and the other hanging down. The sarcophagus was covered with hieroglyphics merely painted, or outlined."*

Unbeknownst to Belzoni at the time, the tomb he discovered belongs to Pharaoh Ramses I, Ramses II's grandfather. After opening a mummy pit on the 13th

Wall reliefs from the tomb of Ramses I (KV 16)

at Gournou- a small tomb with two painted rooms though plundered in the past- on the 16th of October, Belzoni recommenced to finding the sought after royal tomb.

    Belzoni chose a spot fifteen yards away from the tomb of Ramses I to begin digging. Why did he pick a random spot to start digging? Belzoni noticed at the foot of a steep descending hill, a torrent. When it rains, the torrent pours a large quantity of water over one spot and was directing over what could be a tomb. Belzoni was adamant that the spot contained an intact royal tomb. He had the fellahs begin digging from the 16th. On the 18th of October, the fellahs discovered the entrance to the tomb. Belzoni anxiously descended into the interior of the tomb and was bombarded with the most beautiful images to ever be created.

"We perceived the paintings, that the paintings became more perfect as we advanced farther into the interior. They retained their gloss or a kind of

varnish over the colors, which had a beautiful effect."

From there, Belzoni entered a small room coated with more beautiful figures in *basso-relievo* and called the chamber the *Room of Beauties*.

As he traversed the tomb, Belzoni came across a hall with two rows of square pillars coated in hieroglyphics and wall reliefs. Belzoni referred to this room as the *Hall of Pillars*. On the Hall of Pillar's right side contained a small chamber dedicated to the goddess Isis; while on the Pillar's left was named the *Room of Mysteries* due to the mysterious figures. These figures would later be referred to as shabti's; small figures who acted as replacement workers for the individual of the tomb; since it was mandated that everyone in the afterlife had to work. Only those who were buried with shabti escaped this fate.

Another chamber he discovered was the *Apis Room* where Giovanni came across the mummified remains of a bull- who represented the craftsmen

Lithograph of an Apis bull from the tomb of Seti I. Drawn and painted by Giovanni Belzoni

god, Ptah; however, the greatest discovery was the lone sarcophagus at the end of the tomb.

> *"But the description of what we found in the center of the saloon and which have reserved till this place merits the most particular attention, not having its equal in the world, and being such as we had no idea could exist. It is a sarcophagus of the finest oriental alabaster, nine feet five inches long, and three feet seven inches wide....*

Its thickness is only two inches, and it is transparent, when a light is placed in the inside of it....I cannot give an adequate idea of this beautiful and invaluable piece of antiquity, and can only say, that nothing has been brought into Europe from Egypt that can be compared with it."

This tomb belonged to Pharaoh Seti I, father of Ramses II, but at the time of its discovery, Belzoni believed the tomb belonged to a hypothetical pharaoh called 'Psammethis'. Though the tomb didn't contain his mummy, it's considered today amongst Egyptologists to be the finest, largest, and beautifully decorated tomb in the Valley of the Kings. To put it in perspective, Seti I's tomb is long as St. Pauls Cathedral and it was carved in the interior of a mountain! As time went on, Seti I's tomb would be dubbed as *'Belzoni's Tomb'*.

    Sadly, after the discovery of the tomb, the beautifully decorated walls were ruined by a flash flood. Before the flood destroyed the reliefs, Belzoni had drawn the interior of the tomb and made

Seti I before Isis as he holds the "spine" of Osiris (the *Djed Pillar*).

Deir el-Bahri Cache

When Giovanni discovered the tombs of Ramses I and Seti I, the mummies were missing. What happened to them? Where did they go? In 1871, a notorious *'dragoman'* tomb robber named Ahmed Abd el-Rassul, who perhaps was looking for a lost goat that strayed, or, more probably, looking for new "business opportunities," discovered a previously undiscovered tomb at Deir el-Bahri. The blocked entrance at the foot of the steep rock faces at Deir el-Bahri- on the western side bank of the Nile, opposite of Thebes.

As he climbed down the 13m (43ft) shaft, Ahmed found a 70 foot (230 ft) long corridor leading into a hillside. From there, Ahmed, forgetting the stray goat, began to explore the corridors where he discovered not only dozens of shabtis, shabti-boxes, canopic jars, and other funerary equipment, but more importantly, sarcophagi.

The corridor and side chamber were stacked high to the brim with numerous coffins, but these weren't ordinary coffins: these were royal. Numerous

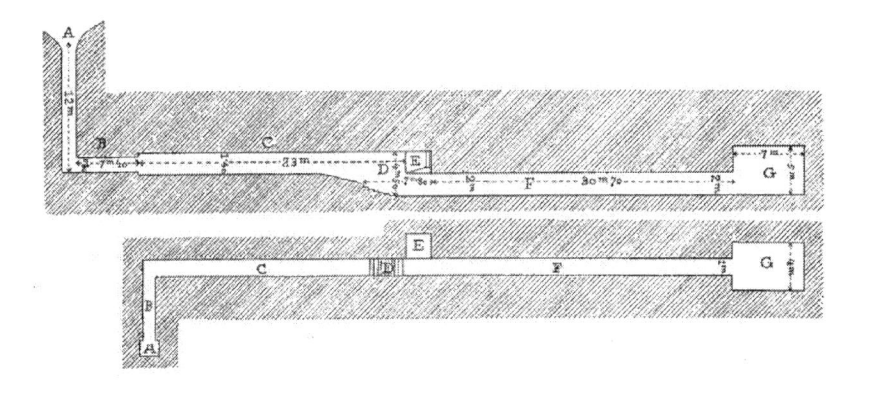

The layout of the Deir el-Bahri Cache tomb

coffins were adorned with the royal golden *uraeus* (cobra). Ahmed had unknowingly made an accidental discovery.

This tomb belonged to the Theban High Priest of Amun-Ra, Pinudjem II (who ruled southern Egypt in the late New Kingdom) and his family. Their coffins still laid in their coffins, untouched for centuries- including their grave goods with six thousand shabti figures stacked. To protect the family in the afterlife.

However, when he gander at the coffins-and possibly thinking of robbing the dead- the majority of the coffins were stripped of any valuable amulets and jewelry that adorned/covered their bodies. After he discovered Tomb DB320, Ahmed enlisted the help of his brothers to gradually remove and leaked the artifacts from the tomb to Luxor's antiquities market. For a time, the Abd el-Rassul family, living comfortably off the proceeds from "their" tomb; until authorities became ever more suspicious that these locals had found a new and important tomb.

What gave the Rassul family away was several important funerary papyri reaching the western market; including objects in the antiquities market. Thus, in 1881 authorities arrested Abd el-Rassul and his younger brother, Hussein, on suspicion of selling artifacts. From there, they were interrogated and tortured by the feared *mudir of Qena*, Daud Pasha, but both bravely refused to give up their secret to the location of the tomb.

But, it was Ahmed's older brother, Mohammed, who knew the jig was up and any further exploitations of the tomb were slim to none. Going against his brother's wishes, Mohammed confessed to Daud Pasha and was rewarded with a hefty sum; ironically, Mohammed would go on to

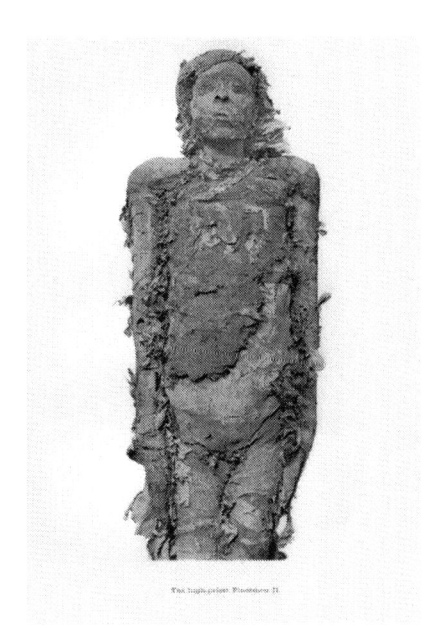

Mummy of High Priest Pinudjem II; the owner of the Deir el-Bahri tomb

securing a job with the Antiquities Service. In the summer of 1881, newly appointed director of Egypt's Antiquities Service, Gaston Maspero ordered his assistant, a man named Emile Brugsch, assistant to investigate this new and exciting tomb.

The mummies collected from the tomb belonged to various queens, pharaohs, lesser royals, and courtiers. The tomb included the mummies of the warrior pharaoh Thutmose III, Amenhotep I, and

Deir el-Bahri Cache

his wife Queen Ahmose Nefertari Ramses I, III, IX, Seti I, and Ramses II.

After unwrapping his body, Maspero discovered the body of Ramses II was well preserved: *"The eyebrows are thick and white, the eyes are small and closed together; the nose is thin and long like the hooked noses of the Bourbons and slightly crushed at the tip by the pressure of the bandages."* Why would some of Egypt's greatest kings be buried in a forgotten tomb? During the tail end of the New

Kingdom, Egypt's vassals in the east were taken by a group from the west known as the *'Sea People'* shrinking Egypt's empire back to its original state.

What made matters worse, Egypt was in financial ruin. Not able to pay the workers, artisans, tomb builders, etc; those who worked in the Valley of the Kings resulted in raiding the tombs of the pharaohs of their precious gold. To ensure the safety of the deceased pharaoh's bodies from being destroyed by the tomb robbers, the priests moved their bodies to a safe and secure location; where they could rest for all eternity.

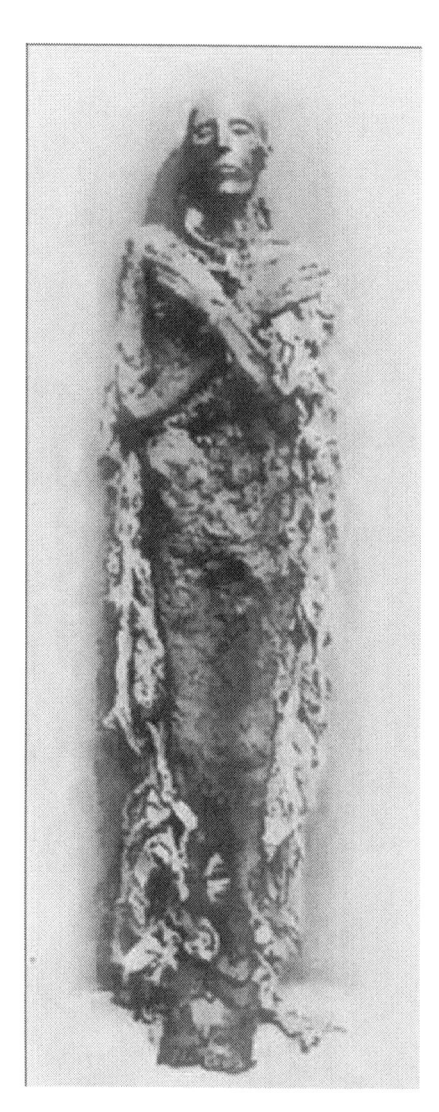

Mummy of Seti I. Discovered at the Deir el-Bahri Cache

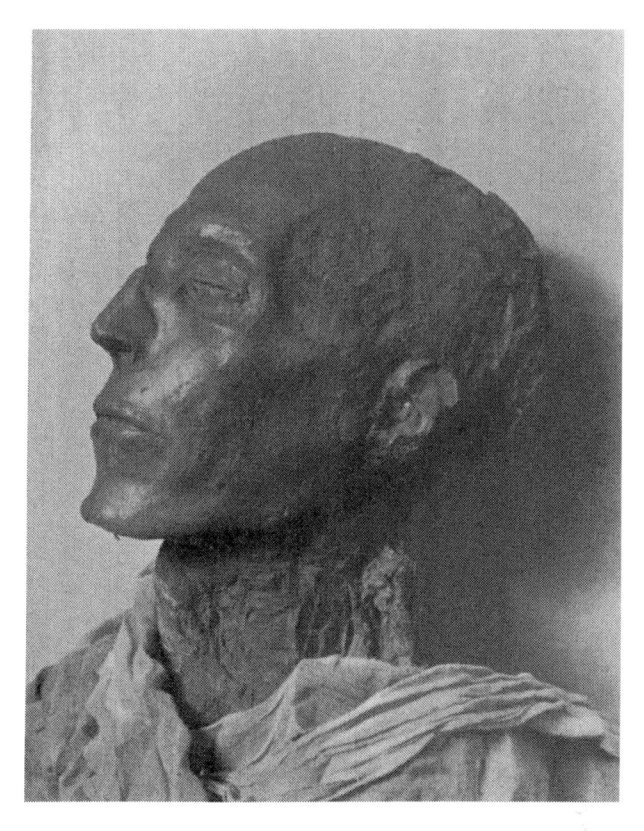

Side view of the mummy of Seti I

(top/bottom) Wall reliefs from the tomb of Seti I. Sketched and painted by Giovanni Belzoni 1817

Lithograph layout of the Tomb of 'Psammethis' (Seti I).
Sketched and painted by Giovanni Belzoni in 1817

(top) Sketched from the tomb of Seti I by Mr. Beechey.
(bottom) The layout of the tomb of Seti I.

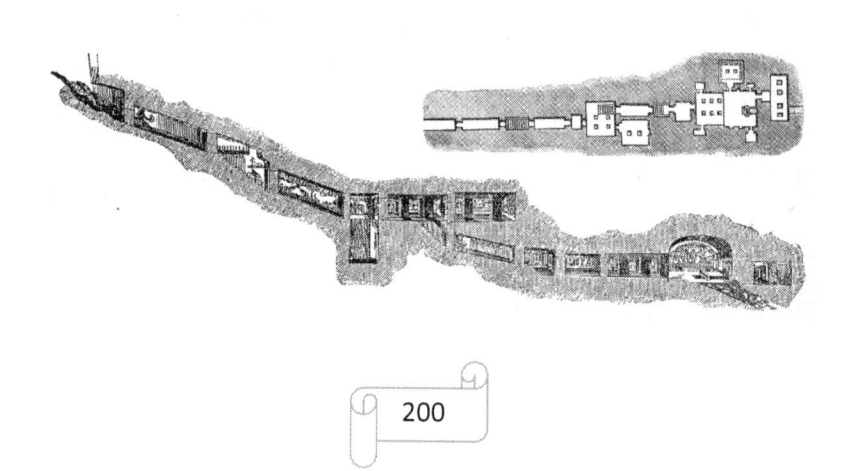

200

Fragment pillar of Seti I before Osiris.

Pharaoh Seti I presenting his offerings before the Djed Pillar ("spine of Osiris")

wax impressions, but the wax impressions and exposure caused damaged as well.

    Having heard the news of Belzoni's latest discovery, Salt rushed to the Valley of the Kings to take a gander for himself. Accompanying him was a touring group of English aristocrats, Lord Bellum and his family, and Salt' biographer. Salt then gave an immediate tour of his tomb despite this being his first time visiting the tomb; all the while ignoring Belzoni who was busily recording the wall reliefs. Belzoni now felt slighted as Salt referred to the tomb as HIS discovery. This set Belzoni off who felt the glory of his accomplishments slipping away.

From that day on, he cut off ties with Mr. Salt and the British consul. When he returned to Cairo, Giovanni went to visit the remainder of his collection being ready to be shipped for the British Museum; only to discover on every sculpture the name of Henry Salt. To make matters worse, Belzoni received journals from Europe about his discoveries, but discovered by Henry Salt as the *"Salt collection"*. '*At this time I received several journals from Europe, and found, to my great surprise, that all my former discoveries and labors had been published in the names of other people, while mine was not even mentioned"*. Belzoni saw this as an act of betrayal from Salt's end and ruined his reputation.

Chapter 11

Opening the Second Pyramid

To correct the injustice brought on to him by Mr. Salt, Giovanni had written an account of his operations in Egypt and gave it to a close confidant Count de Forbin, to be published in French journals; however, this threw more confusion amongst the public since they were getting conflicting accounts of who did what. Seeing his reputation disappear before his very eyes, needed to find a way to enhance his dwindling reputation.

He decided to continue his research by cracking one of Egypt's greatest puzzles on the Giza plateau: the opening to the pyramid of Khefren; however, he wasn't the first to attempt this feat. *"The various attempts which have been made by numerous travelers to find an entrance into this pyramid, and particularly by the great body of French savants, were examples so weighty, that it seemed little short of madness, to think of renewing the enterprise,"* Belzoni told his plan to the Count of trying to uncover the passage and if he succeeded, he would give him a detailed drawing of the pyramid's interior to be sent to France. He had read an account from Herodotus (father of history) that there was no entrance to Khefren's pyramid; however, Giovanni decided to take up the challenge himself to prove if Herodotus' claim was factual and not theoretical. If he found the elusive passage, it would rejuvenate his reputation.

Giovanni headed off to the Giza Plateau and began his investigation. *"I seated myself in the shade of one of those stones on the east side, which forms the part of the temple that stood before the pyramid in that direction. My eyes were fixed on that enormous mass, which for so many ages has baffled conjectures of ancient and modern writers."* After spending time observing the pyramid, Belzoni turned towards the south side. *"With all these thoughts in my mind I arose, and, by a natural impulsion took my walk towards the south side of the pyramid. I examined every part and almost every stone."* As he observed the other sides, Giovanni noticed not all sides of the pyramids looked the same. *"I continued to do so on the west, at last, I came round to the north. Here the appearance of things became to my somewhat different from that at any of the other side."* He began observing the northern side of the pyramid, and didn't find any evidence of an entrance but believed there was an opening.

> *"I observed on the north side of the pyramid three marks, which encouraged me to attempt searching there for entrance into it....I could not conceive how the discovery of the entrance into the second pyramid could be considered as a matter to be despaired of, when no one had ever seen the spot, where it must naturally be presumed to exist..."*

(left) The Pyramid of Khefren (with temple attached to its base) and the Pyramid of Khufu (right)

Satisfied with his observations, he took his case to the Cacheff for men to work on the second pyramid; to which the Cacheff obliged, but Belzoni had to get the go-ahead from the Kakia Bey. Belzoni met the Kakia Bey, who happened to be at Soubra when Giovanni presented his hydraulic machine, to ask permission to excavate the pyramid and got the go-ahead to work on the pyramid.

    Before he could begin, Belzoni had to make his operation a secret from his rivals by keeping quiet. Giovanni began his work on the pyramid's eastern side. As the Fellahs dug and hacked, they came across the lower part of a large temple connected by a portico, to a bigger temple. After days of hacking and removing stone from Khefren's pyramid, the Fellahs, using hatchets to remove the sturdy stone, began to break down from the constant hacking. By this point, Belzoni thought he would find the entrance, but so far there was no sign of the entrance.

He went as far as beginning to doubt himself if he could find it. *"...I was about to become an object of ridicule for making the attempt to penetrate a place..."* To make matters worse, Belzoni had nearly run out of money to pay the Fellahs and would quit if they were sufficiently paid. Giovanni had to rely on a loan from the Briggs and Walmas Bank in Cairo.

With much-needed cash, Belzoni decided to give it one more shot. It was here, Belzoni decided to look back to the Great Pyramid of Cheops (Khufu). He observed the pyramid's entirety and compared it with Khefren's and calculated the entrance had to be nearly thirty feet to the east of the pyramid's northern side. *"I strictly noticed the situation of the entrance into the first pyramid, and plainly saw that it was not the center of the pyramid. I observed that the passage ran in a straight line from the outside of the pyramid to the east side of the king's chamber, and this chamber, being nearly in the center of the pyramid, the entrance consequently must be as far from the middle of the faces the distance from the center of the chamber to the east side of it."*

Satisfied with these new deductions, he had the Fellahs resume work moving stone, but it was during the excavation, Belzoni noticed something. *"I perceived in the excavation a large block of granite, inclining downward at the same angle as the passage into the first pyramid, and pointing towards the center.* From the 28th of February to the 1st of March, Belzoni uncovered what he was looking for. *"...we uncovered three large blocks of granite, tow on each side, and one on the top, all inclined directions towards the center. My expectation and hope increased, as to all appearance, this must prove to be the object of my search."* Then, on March 2, 1818, Belzoni unearthed the

How Did the Egyptians Construct The Pyramids?

The people who built the pyramids were specialists in mathematics, astronomy, and architecture; while the workforce came from Egypt's population. Nearby, settlements were built to house the workers and their families. Once a site was chosen for pyramid construction, surveyors, using a long thick rope, made a mark to where the pyramid would be situated. If the pharaoh was satisfied with the location, he gives his blessing to begin construction.

On the eastern bank of the Nile, workers began mining limestone for the pyramid's exterior. How the workers were able to accomplish this task was not that easy. To remove the hard granite, the workers used wooden wedges and placed them on top of the stone. They soaked the stone with water. All the excess water caused the rock's integral strength to expand and weaken until it splits. The workers then took their copper chisels and placed them and at regular intervals, began the tedious task to remove

Workers tools. Stone hammer and Copper prising tool.

one piece of granite. As soon as they removed the selected piece, the workers took their mallets made out of wood and copper chisel and began chiseling away the sides.

From there they used a set square and plumb line. These two made sure the block was equally leveled, all sides straight and smoothed before being loaded onto sleds. The large stone blocks were then transported onto sleds and tightly tied with long thick rope. Laborers not working in the stone quarries were tasked to push and pull the sled to its final destination ramp. These ramps aided the laborers tremendously. They can haul up the large limestone blocks without using any animals, pulleys! All they had to do was to place the stone in the correct position.

    These ramps, while helpful, could easily cave in on itself due to the weight of the blocks. To ensure the safety of their workers, the ramps were constructed out of mudbrick combined with limestone. While this is going on, workers at Aswan (south of Giza) began the task of cutting and shaping hard granite rock into the pyramid's interior passages, the pharaoh's sarcophagus, and the pyramidion. The pyramidion was a smaller pyramid that acted as the cap to the pyramid. This piece was specially transported to the site by boat. Overall, the pyramids took anywhere from 20 to 30 years and 2.3 million blocks to construct stone wonders.

HERODOTUS. *(Page 148)*

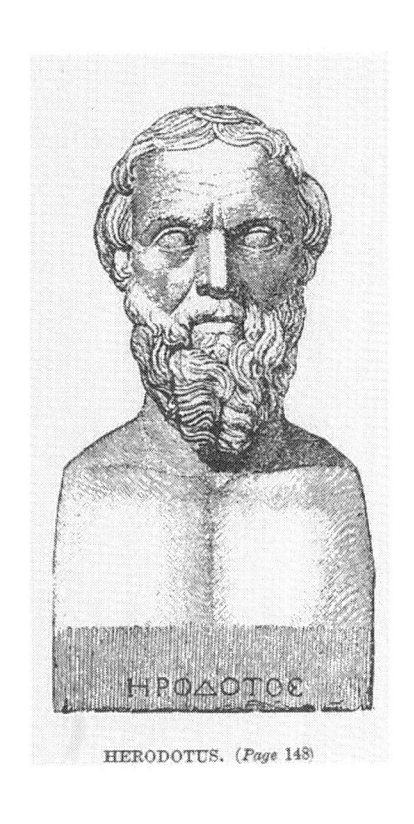

Statue of Herodotus, the Father of History

Lithograph of the entrance to the Pyramid of Khefren.
Sketched and painted lithograph by Giovanni Belzoni

Pharaoh Khefren (2558-2532)

Pharaoh Khefren (or Khafre) was the son of the first builder of the Great Pyramid, Khufu, and was the fourth Pharaoh of the Old Kingdom's fourth dynasty. According to the Turin Royal Canon Papyrus, Khefren ruled Egypt for either 24 or 26 years but was able to produce his very own pyramid. Under his rule, Egypt was prosperous, and what better way to symbolize this time than to build a pyramid. Khefren ordered his pyramid complex to contain a mortuary temple and a valley temple.

The valley temple was constructed out of limestone while its walls were made from red granite., is the oldest structure to survive the modern-day. Within the temple was a statue of Khefren himself; made from diorite, it presented Khefren being protected by Horus (presented as the falcon) on his back while sporting the nemes headdress.

Today, this statue is considered a masterpiece in art. The temple served funerary ceremonies such as purification rituals. The temple even had a

Diorite Statue of Khefren. The protection of Horus helped project the power Khefren had in the mortal world

the passageway leading to the mortuary temple. Khefren's pyramid, when it was fully constructed, was slightly higher than Khufu's. The pyramid standing 447 ½ ft tall, created the illusion of Khefren's pyramid being the tallest of the three Great Pyramids; but since then lost its pyramidion and shrunk by thirty feet.

    The Greek historian Herodotus claimed there was no entrance to Khefren's pyramid, but as we know now, there was an entrance thanks to Giovanni Belzoni's studious observation skills. Khefren's complex contained, arguably its famous, piece, the Great Sphinx. Carved from the leftover limestone from the pyramid of Khufu, the Great Sphinx watches over the Giza plateau as its guardian. The Sphinx contains the body of a lion which represented the sun god Re-Horakhity rising from the east and the guardian of Underworld's western gate.

Theories have ranged the Sphinx is thousands of years older than previously believed to the body of the Sphinx not being that of a lion, but a jackal- if you compared the body of the Sphinx to statues of Anubis in the form of a seated jackal, they eerily have the same body shape and elongated forearms.

The Sphinx today measures at 66ft; while it's length ranges about 240ft. For the majority of its life, the Great Sphinx had been covered in sand, forgotten and uncared for; that is until the New Kingdom when prince Thutmose IV, returning from a hunting trip, grew tired and decided to sleep underneath the head Sphinx. As he slept, the Sphinx came to him in the

The Great Sphinx and Pyramid of Khefren

dream and promises the young prince if he were to remove the sands choking its body, he would make him the next Pharaoh. Thutmose IV honored his request and removed the sands from its body; with the Sphinx honoring his end of the bargain by making Thutmose IV the eighth Pharaoh of the Eighteenth Dynasty. This event was recorded down on a stele referred to today as the *'Dream Stele'* and still resides between the Sphinx's paws.

Lithograph of the opening of the Pyramid of Khefren. Drawn and painted by Giovanni Belzoni

the entrance to the pyramid of Khefren.

> *"I was not mistaken for on the next day, the second of March, at noon, we came at last to the right entrance into the pyramid....Having cleared the front of the three stones, the entrance proved to be a passage four feet high, three feet six inches wide formed of large blocks of graphite, which descended towards the center for a hundred and four-five feet inches at an angle of twenty-six degrees. Nearly all this passage was filled up with large stones, which had fallen from the upper part, and as the passage is inclined downwards, they slid on till some larger than the rest stopped the way.*

Accompanied by Chevalier Frediani, who happened to be traveling the country at the time, Giovanni entered the fabled entrance.

"Before us we had a long passage running in a horizontal direction toward the center. We descended the shaft by means of rope...As my first object was the center of the pyramid, I advanced that way, and ascended an inclined passage, which brought me to a horizontal one, that led towards the center."

As Belzoni and Freniani descended the pyramid, they reached the burial chamber.

"I reached the door at the center of a large chamber....I naturally turned my eyes to the west end of the chamber, looking for the sarcophagus, which I strongly expected to see in the same situation as that in the first pyramid, but I was disappointed when I saw nothing there..."

At first, Belzoni didn't see any evidence of a sarcophagus at the western end of the pyramid, but

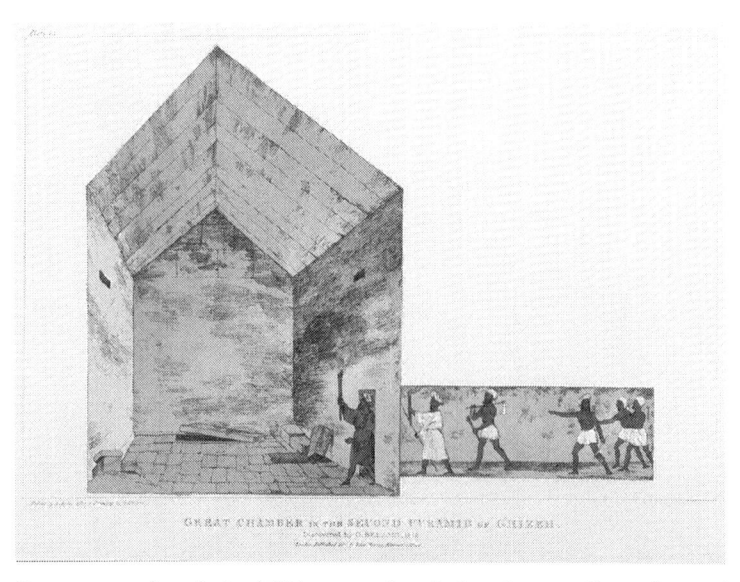

Drawn and painted lithograph of the Great Chamber of Khefren; by Giovanni Belzoni

as he progressed, he discovered the sarcophagus. *"On my advancing toward the west end, I was agreeably surprised to find, that there was a sarcophagus buried on a level with the floor….The sarcophagus is eight feet long, three feet six inches wide, and two feet inches deep in the inside. It is surrounded by large blocks of granite, apparently to prevent its removal, which couldn't be effected without great labor. The lid had been broken at the side so that the sarcophagus was half open. It is of*

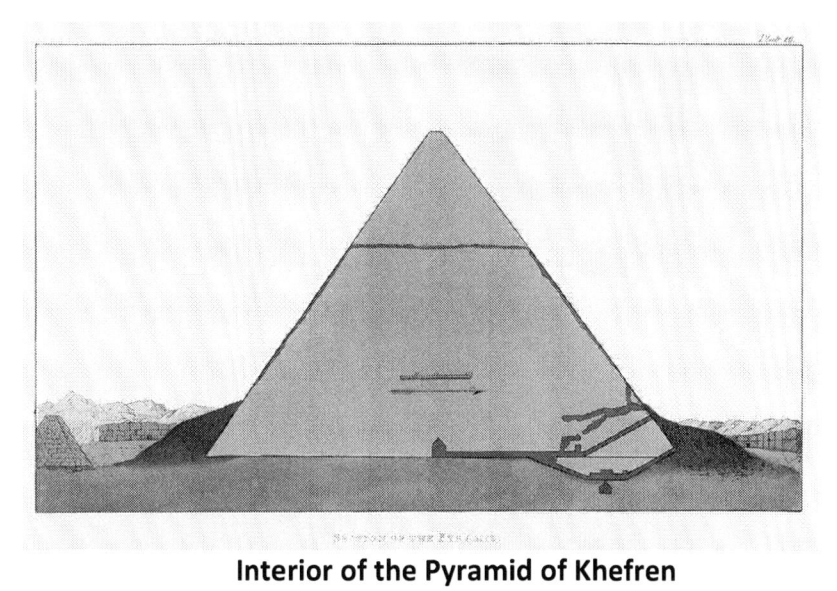

Interior of the Pyramid of Khefren

Were the Pyramids Built By Slaves?

When we think of the pyramids, we instantly image dozens of slaves pulling and dragging limestone blocks as they continuously get whipped by their overseers. This popular image of the pyramid builders stems from the second book in the Bible, the Exodus; in which the Israelites, enslaved for 400 years, were the workforce that constructed some of Egypt's great wonders.

In 450 BC, Herodotus believed the pyramids were constructed by no more than 100,000 slaves. The idea of slaves being responsible for the construction of the pyramids was accepted for thousands of years until late in the Nineteenth Century when archaeologist William Flinders Petrie was excavating a Middle Kingdom pyramid, discovered it was the Egyptian people and not slaves who built the pyramids. Herodotus was wrong.

Roughly 5,000 men worked in the stone quarries, others were either masons or haulers; combined with 20,000 workers who were the cooks, ramp builders, artisans, wood suppliers, the pyramids

The Great Sphinx guarding the pyramid of Khefren

were built by the nation. In the 2000s, pits containing the bodies of the laborers were discovered near the pyramids. To be buried near the pyramid was a privilege to only those who were Egyptian and not of a slave. Within these graves, contained the body-in a fetal position with its head facing north and legs east- of the laborer, and beside him were offerings of beer and bread; so, the deceased had food and drink for the next life.

the finest granite, but like the other in the first pyramid, there is not one hieroglyphic on it."

Despite finding the sarcophagus, Belzoni was dismayed to discover there was nobody inside; however, Belzoni became the first person in four thousand years to walk through the pyramid proving Herodotus' claim of there being no entrance to the pyramid was indeed wrong. *"Herodotus himself was deceived by the Egyptian priests when there were no chambers in it."* Giovanni kept his word and made a detailed plan of the pyramid and passed it on to Count de Forbin to bring back to France.

Belzoni hoped this would finally bring him the recognition he deserved, but when he read from a French newspaper hoping to see his accomplishment, he was shocked to see it was Count de Forbin who discovered the entrance.

> *"On the 24th of April, Mr. Le Comte de Forbin, Director-General of the Royal Museum of France landed at the lazaretto of Marseille….By a happy chance, some days before his departure from Cairo he succeeded in penetrating into the Second*

Pyramid of Giza. Mr. Forbin brings the plans of that important discovery, as well as much information on the labors of Mr. Drovetti at Karnak, and on those which Mr. Salt, the English consul pursues with the greatest success in the Valley of Beben el Malook, and in the plains of Medinet Abu. The Museum of Paris is going to be enriched with some of the spoils of Thebes, which Mr. Forbin has collected in his travels."

Belzoni was angered that once again his accomplishments were being stolen from him by those who didn't even lift a pix ax or moved any stone. Now the people of France and wider Europe would know only of the accomplishments of Drovetti, Forbin, and Salt; however, there is one thing the public doesn't know that Giovanni does.

Upon leaving the pyramid, Giovanni wanted to commemorate this historic event. He went back to the burial chamber and took out from his satchel a large piece of charcoal. Choosing one of the walls, he wrote his name and date: *Opened By. G. Belzoni-*

'Opened By. G. Belzoni- March 2nd, 1818.' Translated from Italian

March 2nd, 1818. Giovanni, after what he had to endure from Mr. Salt, knew his recognition of this moment would be stripped from him and decided to one-up them again. No one, not even Salt, Drovetti, or Forbin was going to take this stolen moment from Giovanni. For the next two hundred years, Belzoni's remained on the wall as a reminder as to who truly discovered the mysterious entrance to the pyramid of Khefren.

Chapter 12

Final Days in Egypt

Despite unearthing the entrance to the pyramid of Khefren, Giovanni would continue his research. When he arrived in Thebes in May 1818 to resume digging, the entire city (each side on the Nile river) was divided between Salt and Drovetti. *"...for if I pointed out any spot in any place whatsoever, one of the parties, I mean the agents of Drovetti or those of Mr. Salt, would consider it as valuable ground and protest that it was taken by them long before."*

With access to Thebes spent, Giovanni decided to take his research to and chose a site abandoned by Salt and Drovetti between the Ramesseum and Medinet Habu. It was here that Belzoni that struck gold once again and discovered another exquisite piece:

"It was perhaps fortune that would have it so, but the fact is, that on the very second day of my researches we came to a large statue, which proved to be the finest of the kind I had yet found….The stone is grey granite….Part of its chin and beard have been knocked off but all the rest is quite perfect."

What Giovanni discovered by chance was the remains of the colossi head of Pharaoh Amenhotep III; who is said to be Egypt's wealthiest, and wisest king in its history.

In that same ground he discovered the Belzoni discovered the colossi head, he uncovered seven more black granite statues of the goddess Sekhmet either sitting or standing. This would be the final discovery Giovanni would make in Egypt.

With every site taken by Drovetti and/or Salt, Belzoni returned to the valley and resumed his wax impressions and sketches of the tomb of Seti I:

"By this time I had taken many impressions of the principal figures in basso-relievo to my entire satisfaction….The great difficulty was to take the impression of the figure without injuring the colors of it….The hieroglyphics in this tomb are nearly five hundred, of which I took a faithful copy, with their colors, but they are four different sizes, from one to six inches so that I have been obliged to take one of each size, which makes nearly two thousand in all."

By this time, Sarah was staying in Jerusalem with Mr. Briggs' family and once he finished his tedious work in the valley, Giovanni would join Sarah; however it was during his work, he met a Frenchmen named Caliud who told him about his travels in the east and what he discovered.

    Caliud, was a silversmith who upon recommended to by Drovetti, was given the task by Muhamad Ali to report on sulfur mines discovered

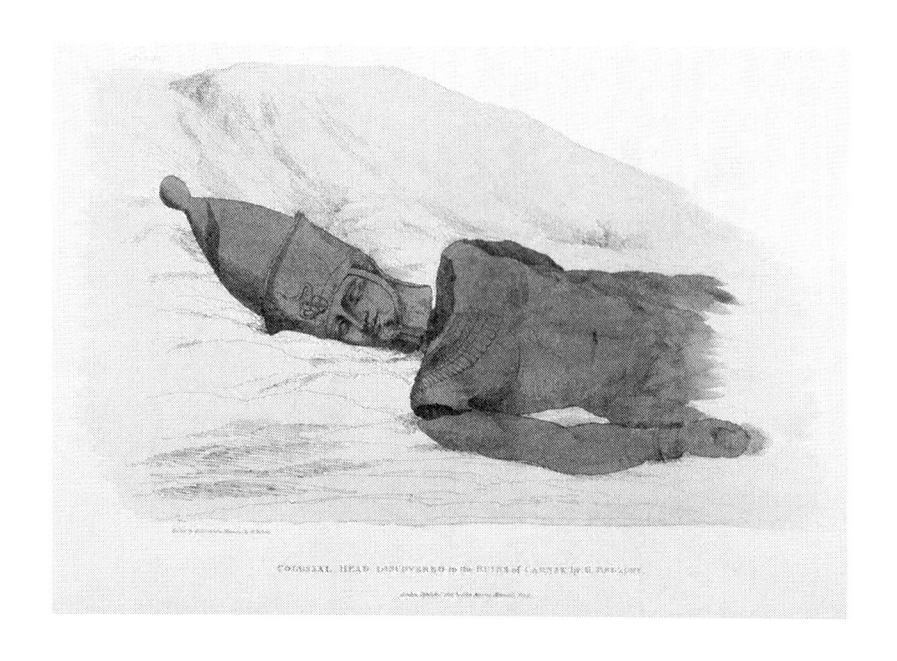

Lithograph of the colossi head of Pharaoh Amenhotep III.
Drawn and painted by Giovanni Belzoni

Lithograph of columns at the King's tombs in Thebes. Drawn and painted by Giovanni Belzoni

in the mountains near the Red Sea. He was accompanied by a special escort of soldiers and miners to the mines; however, when they got there, the sulfur mines were barren.

Not wanting his time there to go to waste, Caliud, instructed personally by Drovtetti, went to visit the ancient emerald mines. upon entering the mines and caves, Caliud discovered emeralds left by the ancient peoples and untouched for centuries. He brought several pieces back to the Pasha as a gift. What intrigued Belzoni the most from Caliud's recollection was the ruins of the ancient city of Bernice.

> " ...Monsieur Caliud gave the account of this place seemed to impress on the minds of antiquaries in Egypt the notion that it must have been the ancient Berenice, especially when he reported it to have eight hundred houses and several temples...that it was near the cost, and that communication with the sea was quite easy".

The colossi head of Pharaoh Amenhotep III discovered by Giovanni Belzoni. Residing today at the British Museum

This was enough to get Belzoni excited to travel once more into the great unknown. As soon as he finished his operation at the Valley of the Kings, Belzoni, accompanied by Mr. Beechey and sixteen camels, left on the 23rd of September to retrace Cailud's steps to find the fabled Berniece.

As they traveled down the Nile, the river was in the stages of Inundation and Giovanni got to see firsthand the power of the Nile river truly had. *"The rapid stream carried off all that was before it, men, women, children, cattle, corn, everything was washed away in an instant and left the place where the village stood without anything to indicate that there had ever been a house on the spot."* Along the way, he came across the Memnoium and its statues rising from the water. *"On our right, we had the high locks and the temple of Gournou, the Memnonium, the extensive buildings at Medinet Abu, and the two colossal statues, which arose out of the water like the lighthouse on some of the coasts of Europe."*

    The statues at the Ramesseum rising out of the river represented the pharaoh, in this case, Ramses II, undergoing his rebirth. As they sailed past the overflooding of the Nile, Belzoni and Beechey made a stop at a place called Wadi Miah. Here, Belzoni discovered the remains of a small temple that was constructed during the reign by Seti I. Once more, Giovanni's life was intertwined with the legacy of the Ramesside Dynasty.

Lithograph of the flooding of the Nile. Drawn and sketched by Giovanni Belzoni

"On our approaching it we were not a little pleased at the sight. It is of small magnitude...it is adorned with Egyptian figures in intaglio relievato, and some retain their color pretty well....At the end of it are three small chambers and there are two others, one at each side, in the corners of the lateral walls, on which are to be seen figures and hieroglyphics in a pretty good style."

Belzoni eventually made his way to Mt. Zabara where he came across the emerald mines Cailud described; only they weren't the mines, but the remains of a mining village. Dismayed not finding the emerald mines and only a village, this didn't stop Belzoni from finding the real city of Berniece. Belzoni decided to head towards the south using D'Anville's map as a guide, where he believed Berniece would be and his belief was rewarded when he discovered the remains of the city half-buried in the sand.

> " Our imagination was so raised by the account of Monsieur Caliud, that I, for my part, expected to distinguish the town by the lofty columns and architecture of some magnificent edifice, or the remains of some high tower, which was to serve me as a guide to the spot.... From the summit where we now were, I expected to have a distant view not only of the sea, but of a wide plain, as it was natural to suppose that a town like Pompeii...

Lithograph of the ruins of Bernice. Drawn and painted by Giovanni Belzoni

> *On our descent, the old man told us, that we should soon see the 'ballet'…. I should have the glorious sight, and indeed the scattered and indeed the scattered and ruined walls of some ancient enclosures announced to us, that we should soon see some habitation. I observed a square hole in the rock, which had evidently been cut by some of the miners in form of a chapel, as before mentioned."*

But before he could observe t ruins, Belzoni was running low on food and water and had to return to Egypt; though he did stop at the site of Saiket where he observed a small Greek Temple. Even though Belzoni was not able to excavate the site of Berniece, in his eyes was a success nonetheless; while others believed to be a financial disaster.

On his return to Egypt in November 1818, there was still the issue of removing the obelisk at Philae. Belzoni arrived at Philae on the 16th to begin the arduous process of removing the obelisk from its

Pharaoh of the Exodus?

The second book in the Old Testament, The Book of Exodus, tells the story of Moses, being called by God through the burning bush after years of his people crying out to Him for deliverance, to deliver his people, the Hebrews, out of Egypt and bring them to the Promise Land. In the story, Moses goes up to the Pharaoh and delivered the most famous words in the Bible" *"Let My People Go."* But the Pharaoh's heart was hardened and refused to free Moses' people.

This act resulted in Moses, through the power of God, to send 10 terrible plagues to the land of Egypt; with each plague being worse than the last. It was only the last plague, the *Death of the Firstborn* when his firstborn son died by the hand of God, that finally broke through to the Pharaoh's hardened heart and gave the Hebrews their freedom.

The Pharaoh is never named in the story, but many scholars and historians believe the Pharaoh of the Exodus was Ramses II. How did they come to this conclusion? In Exodus, tells us, the reader, how

"Let My People Go." Moses and his brother Aaron before the Pharaoh.

Ramses' palace at Pi-Ramesses was built not by Egyptians but by the Israelites. *"There arose up a new king over Egypt, which knew not Joseph, and he said unto his people 'Behold! The people of the children of Israel are more and mightier than we are...' Therefore they did set over them taskmasters to afflict them with their burdens. And they built for the Pharaoh treasure cities, Pithom and Raamses... "*

By the time of Ramses II, the population of Egypt grew exponentially with the inclusion of minorities or foreigners who had settled in the Delta; however, there is no record of any mass enslavement of Israelites and if there was one, it was either destroyed or lost to time. Historically, minorities and foreigners living in Egypt were summoned to work under the Egyptian state. After Moses and the Hebrews left Egypt for the Promise Land, the Pharaoh changed his mind and went after them.

    Moses and the Hebrews stopped at the Red Sea; were on the opposite side was freedom. At the moments of freedom, the Pharaoh's army had caught up to them. In their desperate hour, Moses called to God to help them. God instructed Moses to move to the sea. *"And Moses stretched out his hand over the sea, and the Lord caused the sea to go back by a strong east wind all that night, and made the sea dry land, and all the waters were divided. And the children of Israel went into the midst of the sea upon the dry ground: and the waters were a wall unto them on their right hand, and on their left. And the Egyptians pursued and went in after them to the midst of the sea, even all Pharaoh's horses, his chariots and his horsemen...And Moses stretched forth his hand over the sea, and the sea returned to his strength...and the waters returned and covered*

Lithograph of Moses parting the Red Sea

the chariots and the horsemen, and all the hosts of Pharaoh that came into the sea after them; there remained not so much as one of them." Despite the lack of evidence, Ramses II is considered by the public, as the Pharaoh of the Exodus.

resting place. Belzoni was able to get the obelisk as far up the Nile, but as it reached the pier Belzoni constructed for this task, the pier caved in causing the obelisk to slide off into the Nile! With the obelisk seemingly gone, all hope seemed lost, yet Belzoni was unfazed by this hurdle.

> "I caused a great quantity of stones to be brought to the waterside. I then desired several men to enter the water, and to make a heap of stone on the ide of the obelisk opposite to the shores and to form a solid bed for the levers to rest upon....Two ropes were passed under the obelisk: that end which was from under it was fastened to some date trees....Having set the men at the rope to pull, and those of the divers to mount the extremities of the levers, the obelisk rose on the side opposite the bank, and when the levers were to be removed, the obelisk was propped by stones under it."

Ramses The Peacemaker

After the "defeat" of the Hittites at the Battle of Kadesh, Ramses II knew it was only a matter of time before the Hittites would attack their vassal states. However, a new power was beginning to rise in the east: the Assyrians. The Assyrians began invading Hittite territory and slowly chipping away territory. They invaded the Hittite territory for a second time and now found themselves in greater danger than ever before. The only thing separating the Hittites from an open invasion from the Assyrians was the Euphrates river and the Hittite king, Hattusili, wasn't going to ally with the Assyrians.

Hattusili had no other choice but to explore a possible peace with their hated enemy Ramses II. After a year of back and forth bickering and negotiations, in December 1259 BC, ten years after the Battle of Kadesh a treaty was forged between both superpowers. Delegates from the Hittite empire made their way to Per-Ramses where they bowed before Ramses and presented the "God-Pharaoh" a silver engraved cuneiform tablet. This tablet, a gift from Hatsulli himself, was a copy of the lengthy treaty that now and until the end of time, bound the Egyptians and Hittites as mutual friends and allies. Not to pass up an opportunity when he saw it, Ramses II had the treaty carved on the walls of Ipetsut as a symbol of his great diplomatic skills. This is what the quote says:

> *'Behold, Hattusili, the ruler of the Hittites, binds himself by treaty to Usermaatra, chosen-one-of-Ra, the great ruler of Egypt, beginning today, so that perfect peace and brotherhood may be created between us forever-he being in brotherhood and peace with me, and I being in brotherhood and peace with him, forever.'*

This treaty was a nonaggression pact, a defensive alliance against the Assyrians, both sides allow amnesty for refuges, safeguard rightful succession in both nations; with honor on both sides could claim victory. Ramses II then gave up any aspirations of conquering Amurru but retained his rights in both Lebanese and Syrian ports as far as Ugarit.

With the signing of the treaty, the Near East was at peace for the first time since the golden days of Amenhotep III. This treaty would go down in the history of mankind as the world's first peace treaty between two superpowers. Today, you can still see the remnants of the treaty on the walls of Karnak and the Ramesseum and the Hittite version on clay tablets. Not wanting to be the one who sued for peace, both Ramses II and Hatsulli fabricated the account that they were the ones who wanted; i.e. the Hittites account states it was Ramses who sued for peace and not the Hittites. This peace would last until the collapse of the New Kingdom

Sideview of the mummy of Ramses II

It appears Belzoni had done another impossible feat and successfully retrieved the obelisk thanks in part to his engineering skills.

Once properly securing the obelisk to the boat, Belzoni set sailed to Karnak. There was fear of the obelisk's weight would cause the boat to collapse inwards and sink; plus the obelisk, if the boat made fast turns or hit something, could've caused damage to the obelisk. The obelisk arrived safely in Karnak. Today, the obelisk resides at the Kingston Lacy estate in Dorset, England.

When Belzoni arrived at Karnak with the obelisk, Drovetti was furious to see the Paduan taking the claim to what was considered his. Drovetti got into a heated argument with Belzoni over the ownership of the obelisk. He claimed that he found the obelisk at Philae and laid claim to it way before Belzoni got into Egypt. Drovetti went as far as accusing Giovanni of illegally stealing it from him. This jealously didn't stop between both parties. Drovetti had his agents locate and violently beat Giovanni's servant, James. He taunted him and threatened him with more violence as they pointed their armed rifles at Belzoni as a reminder.

The matter was eventually settled; there was no evidence the obelisk belonged to Drovetti for his agents never made it to the island of Philae and since he moved the obelisk himself, belonged to Giovanni. Despite winning his case against Drovetti, it became clear for Belzoni it was no longer safe to work in Egypt.

> *"...it was a high time for me to quit the country, so I returned to Beben el Malook, and immediately commenced my preparations to depart for Europe, for I, could not live any longer in a country where I had become the object of revenge... notwithstanding the advantages, I might have derived in the continuation of my researches..."*

From there, Giovanni began the tough task of removing the fragile alabaster sarcophagus of Seti I, from its tomb, but there was an unforeseeable accident.

> " I was then making a canal to turn the course of the water, that it might not run into the tomb was situated under a small torrent of water….The consequence was, that while I was absent up the Nile it happened to rain the water, finding the entrance open, ran into the tomb, and though not much, was enough to cause some damage to some of the figure…but I fear, that in the course of a few years it will become much worse, and I am persuaded, that the damp in the rainy days has caused as much damage in the tombs."

As the field of Egyptology expanded in the nineteenth century, Egyptologists would condemn Belzoni as responsible for destroying much of the tomb of Seti I. for now though, Giovanni was able to secure the sarcophagi onto a boat; however, as much as he

A modern recreation of an Egyptian Obelisk. Located at the Rosicrucian Museum, San Jose, CA.

wanted to return to Europe, Belzoni had to first stop at Alexandria to testify in court for the incident at Luxor over the obelisk and Drovetti. *"I was glad to see that my cause had been taken up, but I was in very little hopes…"*

When Belzoni arrived in Alexandria, Drovetti was protesting to the courts against this unlawful lawsuit towards himself and his agents. He went as far as accusing Mr. Salt of the lawsuit, to begin with, but Salt wasn't in Alexandria to make his case. The court had to postpone proceedings until Salt returned from Upper Egypt. In the meantime decided to take one final journey in Egypt.

> *"For a long time, I had a wish to make a small excursion into the western desert. I had observed that the temple of Jupiter Ammon had been an object of search for a long time, and by more than one traveler, but that the true spot where it existed had not been fixed."*

The temple of Jupiter Ammon is famous today for its oracle who told the Macedonian conqueror, Alexander the Great, that he was indeed divine and legitimize him as Pharaoh of all Egypt. The deity, Jupiter Ammon, was the fusion between two different deities: the Greek god of thunder, lightning, the sky, and king of all the Olympian gods, Zeus, and the Egyptian god, Amun. He is represented as a man with rams horns.

Giovanni left the town of Rosetta on the 20th of April, 1819, and set off for the Faiyum. Unfortunately for Sarah, Belzoni still felt she would be in danger, and decided to leave her in Rosetta near the British agency. On the 29th, He took a boat and headed straight to Beni Suef, a town eighty miles south of Cairo. From there, Giovanni entered the Faiyum.

As he traversed the Faiyum, Belzoni made his way to Lake Qarun where he discovered an ancient labyrinth described by Herodotus and Strabo, but before he entered, he was nearly mauled by a hyena! *"I was mounting the few steps that lead to the platform of the small chapel, a large hyena rushed from the apartments beneath the chapel…the animal stopped three or four yards from me, and then turned around as if determined to attack me, but appeared on second thoughts to have relinquished its intent, and after having shown me its pretty teeth, gave a hideous roar, and set off galloping as fast as it could."*

It appears once again, luck seemed to follow the giant. After the hyena finished laughing at Belzoni, the adventurer entered the labyrinth.

> *" The Labyrinth was a building of 3,000 chambers one half above and one half below. The construction of such an immense edifice, and the enormous quantity of materials which must have been accumulated....The town was about a mile in circumference, with the temple in its center, so that I could not see how the Labyrinth could be placed in this situation."*

There is confusion as to whether Giovanni discovered an actual labyrinth; however, the term labyrinth described by classical scholars meant temple complex. What Belzoni discovered was the Hawara temple complex dating as far back to the 12th dynasty. A few days later, Giovanni decided to

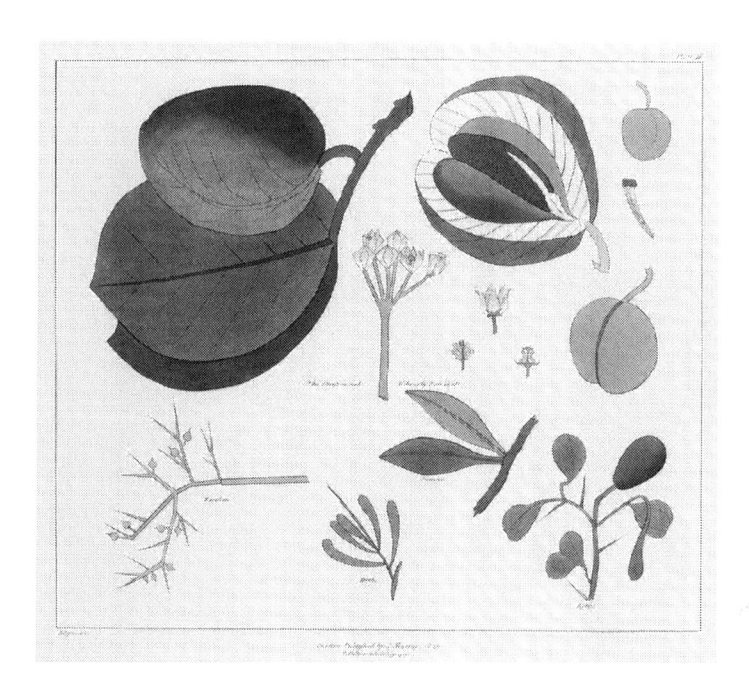

Lithograph of tropical plants. Drawn and painted by Giovanni Belzoni

explore the western tip of the lake where he came across the town of the Greek god of wine Dionysius.

> "...I perceived the ruins of a town not far distant. On my arrival, I found it to be a Greek town, and it cannot be any other than the city of Bacchus, which I have observed in some of the maps of

ancient authors. There are a great number of houses, half tumbled down, and a high wall of sun-burnt bricks, which encloses the ruins of a temple....There is a causeway, or road, made of large stones, which runs through the town to the temple, which faces the south..."

On the sixth of May, Giovanni returned to the Faiyum and began preparing for his search of the Oasis of Jupiter of Ammon.

    Before he set off, Belzoni decided to stop and see the ruins of Arsinoe. *"It had been a very large city, but nothing of it remained, except high mounds of all sorts of rubbish. The chief materials appear to have been burnt bricks."* For the next twelve days, Belzoni left the village of Sedinin and entered the desert. Traveling by a small caravan, Giovanni headed west and encountered the ruins of Kaweje Tutan. *"I saw a great many blocks of calcareous stone with hieroglyphics and Egyptian figures very finely executed and some pedestals of columns."* Along the way, he passed the ruins of el-Garak el-Sultani, and

Ancient Greek coin of Zeus Ammon; notice the ram's horn on the side indicating the fusion between Greco and Egyptian deities

finally Ain el-Ruwayan. Still heading west to the Oasis, on the 19th, Belzoni passed through the wadi called Bahr-Balama (*"The Valley of the river without water"*). Here, Giovanni believed the areas rocky edifice belonged to the tomb of Greek general Cambyses' 50,000 army that perished in the desert.

> *" It will be recollected, that Cambyses, after having conquered Egypt sent part of his army to the conquest of the Ammonii in the deserts of Libya, which was betrayed by their guides, who were Egyptians, and left to perish in the desert, and nothing more was heard of them."*

Despite believing this site belonging to Cambyses' troops, Belzoni couldn't go further with his theory; since his traveling troupe was running low on water and had to return to camp to refill.

On the 25th, after six days of traveling, Belzoni arrived at the oasis of Bahariya (oasis of El Cassar). It was here, the Paduan believed he found the Oasis of

Jupiter Ammon. Giovanni deduced this to be the spot due to the Bedouin encampment that founded a spring that was cold during the day and warm at night. According to the ancient accounts, this spring was called the Fountain of the Sun and was near the Temple of Jupiter; however, the area where Belzoni thought was the Oasis of Jupiter Ammon was the Oasis of Siwa.

Content with his discovery, Belzoni made the long trek back to Beni Suef and arrived on the 15th of June. From there, he traveled to Rosetta to pick up Sarah, but along the way had to contend with the onset of plague and had to self-quarantine. On the 23rd, Giovanni now reunited with Sarah decided it was time to leave Egypt for good and return home.

Chapter 13

Return to Europe

After spending five years in Egypt, Giovanni and Sarah arrived in Venice in November 1819. Upon their arrival, Belzoni hoped to receive a hero's welcome, but instead, he and Sarah had to be placed under quarantine. Europe was still pronged to get the plague and due to their time in Egypt, they may have picked up the plague and could easily spread it to the populace. Though they were stuck in quarantine, Belzoni did receive a hero's welcome from the *Gazzetta privilegtia of Venice* as the *"celebrated traveler Belzoni."* The fear of his exploits being forgotten was put at rest for Belzoni. His feats were known to his country and his hometown of Padua.

On the 6th of December, Giovanni and Sarah were released from quarantine and made their way to Padua. During his time at Padua, Belzoni met up with his family as he recounted to them the dangers he had to overcome, how he moved the head of the *Younger Memnon* with his hands; how he moved the sands choking the temple at Abu Simbel, and how he discovered the long-forgotten chamber of the Second Great Pyramid. All the while, showing his drawings of the ancient monuments.

Before he left his hometown for the final time, Giovanni stopped by the old café shops and retold his adventures to returning sailors like they did when he was a lad and the townspeople who wanted to meet their hero. Upon his departure, Belzoni donated two statues of Sekhmet (from Karnak) to be placed at the *sala della ragione* (marketplace) for everyone to admire. In return for his gracious gift, the city gave the giant a medal with stricken images of Sekhmet.

Giovanni and Sarah stayed in Padua for a few months and in early February 1820, Belzoni and Sarah left Padua and set sail for England. On the 31st of March, Belzoni and Sarah arrived in England with the English Times recording *"the celebrated traveler Mr. Belzoni has arrived in this metropolis after an*

Statue of the Goddess Sekhmet. Still resides at Padua's Sala Dello Ragione

absence of 10 years, 5 of which he has employed in arduous researches after the curious remains of antiquities in Egypt and Nubia." It appears that the recognition Belzoni was hoping for seemed to come to pass. Everyone now knew it was he who moved the Memnon and not Salt; and his research was acknowledged for the first time. Both the alabaster sarcophagus and the Philae obelisk were at the port of Alexandria ready to be exported to England.

While he was in England, Belzoni was planning to take his drawings and wax sculptures from the tomb of Seti I and recreate the pharaoh's tomb as a "final resting place" for the sarcophagus; however, there was still the issue of his reputation. Although he had gained a status for moving the colossi amongst the general populace, the collection he amassed for the British Museum was still seen as the 'Salt Collection'. To rectify this issue, Belzoni, from the moment he landed in Great Britain, went to work on writing the memoirs of his accomplishments, passion, failures, research, and the culture of Egypt and Nubia from his perspective.

In late 1820, Belzoni published his account entitled *"Narrative of the Operations and Recent Discoveries Within the Pyramids, Temples, Tombs, and Excavations, in Egypt and Nubia And of a Journey to the Coast of the Red Sea in Search of the Ancient*

Portrait of Giovanni Belzoni by Jan Adam Kruseman (1824)

Berenice and Another to the Oasis of Jupiter Ammon." The Narrative goes over Belzoni's travels into three parts- known as the "3 Journeys"- with the final being an account from Sarah's perspective of her time in Egypt; titled *"The Women of Egypt, Nubia, and Syria."*

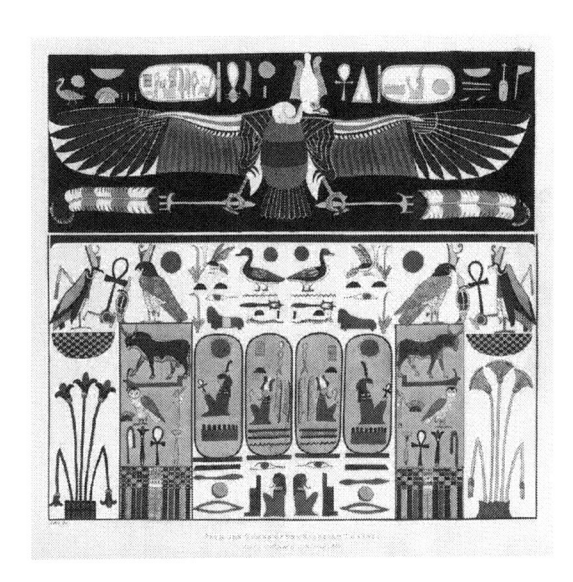

(top) Lithograph of Bird representation. (bottom) Lithograph from the tomb of Seti I. Drawn and painted by Giovanni Belzoni

(top) Lithograph of Osiris and the gods. (bottom) Lithograph of Isis. Drawn and painted by Giovanni Belzoni

Within the massive volume, contained an atlas of Egypt, beautiful watercolor lithographs from Belzoni of his travels throughout Egypt and Nubia. Upon its release, the Narratives was a resounding critical and financial success; with one review proclaiming Belzoni "*...he may justly be considered as the pioneer, and a most powerful and useful one, of antiquarian researches; he points out the road and makes it easy for others to travel over...*" Due to the commercial success of the Narratives, it went back for a second (1821), then the third edition in (1823). These editions were then translated into German, French, and Italian.

In the Narratives, Belzoni recounts his entire journey in Egypt and Nubia as describes how he accomplished his feats by himself and not by Mr. Salt, and painting the image of the culture and daily life of Egypt and Nubia; however, not everyone knew who Belzoni was or looked like. Sure, some know Belzoni during his tenure as the *Patagonian Sampson*, but many were unaware of the giant. Belzoni's response was to tease the public more

Portrait of Henry Salt. 1815

about Ancient Egypt. Belzoni had brought back with him one of the mummies from the Valley of the Kings and unwrapped them before doctors and medical students. The last time Belzoni performed in front of a large crowd was when he was the Patagonian Sampson, now he was before the Royal College of Surgeons unveiling the first unwrapped mummy in

Unwrapping Mummies

Although Giovanni unwrapped a mummy before the Royal College Surgeons, he was not the first one to do so. In ancient times, tomb robbers raiding tombs of the pharaohs would unwrap the mummies looking for any trinkets of gold and violently ripped them off the mummies; but not before scattering the broken mummy remains. By the time of the Middle Ages, the art of mummification had been lost to European knowledge; however, during the Renaissance, there was renewed interest in the art of mummification.

The only problem being, there were few mummies to study from since most of the bodies were grounded up into medicine by the Persians called *Mummia*. The Persians used the mummia only for the king and it was believed the remains had special healing powers such as healing cuts or mending broken bones within minutes. For centuries, the Persians valued mummia over gold itself. The Europeans, hearing the word mummia from travelers, applied the name to the preserved bodies.

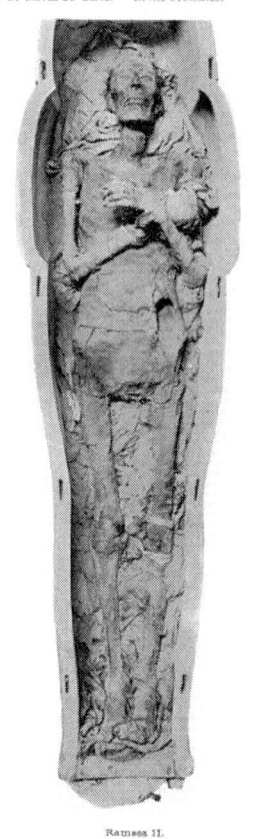

Unwrapped mummy of Ramses II

By the Seventeenth and Eighteenth centuries, mummia became a hot commodity for European medicine; however, they imported mummia from Persia where it became rarer by the day.

The best source of mummia for Europeans came from Egypt. Resin coating the ancient bodies acted as a source of the mummia mineral. Soon, Europeans began traveling to Egypt where they were given mummies for scientific study. One of the first recorded unwrapping of an Egyptian mummy was in 1718 by Christian Hertzog. The unwrapped mummy was headless, but within its bandages contained seventy-four amulets in perfect condition. By the late Eighteenth Century, mummy unwrapping became more frequent and quite popular amongst physicians. At the tail end of the century, Napoleon Bonaparte's team too acted on unwrapping mummies.

Bonaparte's team, when they weren't fighting, found mummies still sleeping in their tombs. They took them out and dissected them and it was here where they began to observe and record different wrapping techniques for mummification; with some going far as noting the removal of the brain. However, some of the soldiers would decapitate the heads of mummies and send them back to Europe; thus destroying the identity of the individual. The importance of unwrapping mummies helped shed light and confirm ancient texts from Herodotus and Diodorus about the art of mummification; those being the style of wrapping the mummies, the black thick resin coating the mummies body for preservation, and the anatomical feats such as accurately removing the internal organs.

    Unwrapping mummies became so popular, that for a time, became a popular pastime. For instance, in Victorian England, the noble class would throw parties over unwrapping a single or a dozen mummies for the fun of it! Thomas Pettigrew was famous for unwrapping mummies at these parties and would unwrap one or two mummies before everyone. But like all crazes, unwrapping mummies became tired and old and soon faded into obscurity.

(top) Lithograph from the tomb of Seti I. (bottom) Lithograph at the Temple of Offendia, Nubia. Drawn and painted by Giovanni Belzoni

At Picadilly, Belzoni created his Egyptian hall containing his collection of Egyptian artifacts, drawings of Seti I, recreations from his tomb, statues of Sekhmet, mummies, the ram-headed sphinx's, the papyri, and a small scale model of the Pyramid of Khefren. On the grand opening on the 1st of May 1821, Belzoni appeared before the anxious public wrapped up like a mummy as he shambled his body at the scared masses! Thousands came to see the artifacts up close, but the biggest attraction was Belzoni himself. He would give grand enthusiastic tours of the exhibit, recounting his stories and ordeals in showman fashion.

Soon after the opening, the invitations went out to illustrious personalities such as Augustus Fredrick and Sir Walter Scott, to the Duke of Sussex; who was the sixth son to King George III. Everyone wanted to be around the giant, get to know him. In 1822, Belzoni traveled to Russia where he met with Czar Alexander I at his palace in Petersburg and recognition of his feats, personally gave the giant a topaz ring. What Giovanni desperately desired was recognition from academics. When he returned to

(top) Lithograph of The Temple of Dakke, Nubia. (bottom) Lithograph The ruins of Karnak. Drawn and painted by Giovanni Belzoni

Lithograph of the Temple of Erments. Drawn and painted by Giovanni Belzoni

(top) Lithograph of a procession. (bottom) Lithograph of Ethiopian procession. Drawn and painted by Giovanni Belzoni

279

London in June 1822, his Egyptian exhibit at Piccadilly, once the grand attraction in the country, was now closed. He appealed to the British Museum to buy the Belzoni Collection, but the museum wasn't that interested. In their eyes, they already had the best collection deposited by Mr. Salt. Not even his research was taken into consideration amongst academics.

Giovanni was forced to sell off his entire collection in auctions just to make ends meet. Not wanting to be forgotten by the populace, Belzoni tried to recreate his success at Piccadilly this time in France; however, his second time ended as soon as it began. And then it was over. Egypt mania, like all manias, ceased to be. Giovanni was now forgotten and was replaced by new acts of the day.

Chapter 14

The Final Adventure

Belzoni was now in dire financial straights. He didn't discover any treasures at Abu Simbel or the second pyramid to sell off to and the alabaster sarcophagus hadn't arrived yet to sell to a potential buyer. To reclaim public attention and needed finances, Belzoni looked back to Africa. He had unlocked Egypt's secrets but now wanted to find its heart.

During his time with Burkhardt, Belzoni learned about the mythical and forgotten city called Timbuktu. He felt the call of adventure calling out to him for one last time. With just enough money from his shows at Piccadilly, Belzoni and Sarah traveled to Africa in late 1822. They landed in Morocco and as Belzoni headed to the town of Fez, Sarah decided she

Mali Empire

  The forgotten city of Timbuktu Giovanni was desperately looking for once belonged to the Mali Empire. From the 13th to the 17th century, Mali initiated great influence and culture over West Africa. The Mali kings, called *'Mansa,'* could trace their lineage back to the first king, Sundiata Keita. Dubbed *"The Lion King,"* Sundiata, united the smaller Malinke kingdoms after capturing the empire of Ghana in 1240. Under the reign of Mansa Musa I, Mali would see the longest territorial expansion and innovations in architecture.

  With a large army, Musa doubled the empire which allowed Mali to enjoy the benefits of being the center of trade in the entirety of Africa. Since Musa was Muslim, he undertook a pilgrimage to Mecca in 1324. It was during this pilgrimage, where Musa spent and gave away his gold that generated stories of the unlimited wealth Mali had in their possession. The city of Timbuktu itself became a center of all knowledge of the region. What put Mali on the map for eager European explorers was the Spanish cartographer Abraham Cresques who created an image of Musa wearing a golden crown as he held gold in his hand. This image solidified Timbuktu as a city of gold and it's accepted amongst historians and scholars that Musa was the richest king in history.

His influence can be still felt today in the region's universities, schools, Islamic learning centers, and the grand library; all thanks to Musa's influence over the region. In the wake of his death in 1337, the once-great empire's influence over Africa slowly began to deteriorate. New trading centers began popping up around the country that took away goods and gold Mali once enjoyed freely.

From there, a period of weaker kings gave way to numerous civil wars until the late 15th century when the neighboring Songhay Empire sacked Timbuktu; leaving behind the remnants of a great empire. By the time Giovanni entered the country, Mali had been absorbed into the Moroccan Empire.

Cartographer Abraham Cresques image of Mansa Musa I; the richest king in history

(top) Terracotta statue of a Mali Equestrian (13th-17th).
(bottom) Timbuktu astronomical and mathematical manuscripts.

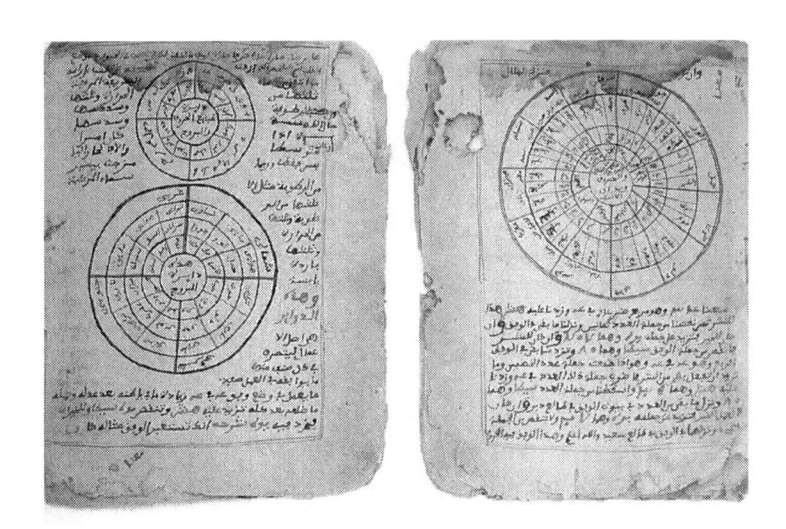

The City of Timbuktu

The city of Timbuktu (1830)

had enough of adventures and boarded a ship and returned to Great Britain. This would be the last time she'll ever see her husband.

Now alone, Belzoni set out and reached the Cape Coast on the 15th of October. From there, Belzoni made it to the Benin river (modern Nigeria). In November 1822, Belzoni planned to travel northward the Benin river to the town of Houssa, and on the 22nd, he sailed up the Benin river; however,

Map of Timbuktu

this area was known for its endemic diseases. Belzoni had gotten lucky in Egypt, but now he was older and he couldn't escape the same fate that struck down explorers traveling the region.

At the village of Gwato, Belzoni complained of abdominal l pain, then suffered an intense intestinal attack. On the 3rd of December 1822, Giovanni Belzoni, the gentle giant of Padua, dies of dysentery. He was only forty-five years old. He was buried six feet underneath a large tree with three salvos. Five years later, on July 4th, 1827, Padua erected a giant statue of Belzoni as an honor to his greatest discoveries; however, his collection at the British Museum is still remembered as the Salt Collection.

Chapter 15

Legacy

Giovanni Belzoni has been condemned by modern Egyptologists as nothing more than a treasure hunter. Despite making incredible discoveries in Egypt, moving the Younger Memnon, and removing the sands from Abu Simbel, he is viewed as a raider raiding the tombs of Ancient Egyptians for quick and easy money; while others claim him to be an amateur archaeologist' whose over the top methods did more harm to the ancient culture than good. The field of Egyptology was in its early infancy during Belzoni's time and raiding the tombs and sites of antiquities was not only preferable but acceptable.

However, due to continual competition between rival factions, resulted in priceless antiquities being defaced or destroyed so no one could claim it for their own. Belzoni let alone

Drovetti didn't know the ancient hieroglyphics on statues and wall reliefs across Egypt was a spoken language; they just saw the antiquities as nothing more than a job as the demands for Egyptian antiquities from two of Europe's prestige Museums, the Louvre and British Museum were in high demand. This didn't help quell the continuous raiding of Egypt's antiquities.

Though he has been perceived as a treasure hunter, Belzoni was anything but that. Giovanni Belzoni is considered one of the earliest pioneers of modern Egyptology. For instance, while Drovetti was raiding Egypt's sites of antiquities, Belzoni took his time to observe, record, and draw the sites as they were for the past three thousand years. Why would he, an "amateur" and tomb raider, take time to carefully observe the ancient monuments if he was too busy raiding tombs?

Belzoni grew to love Egypt's ancient past and though he wasn't an "expert" his mindset as an archaeologist and Egyptologist was there. He even

Portrait of Giovanni Belzoni

went as far as learning and adopting Arabic culture; something rare for a European in those times.

Sure, his methods were outlandish, and yes he may have accidentally crushed mummies due to the bad air, but it was his keen observation skills, that allowed him to discover some of the most beautiful tombs in the Valley of the Kings, the long-sought opening to the Second Pyramid; something no "expert" could've accomplished on their own.

Let's not forget that Giovanni nearly died on different occasions and yet he still went on to do great things. All the struggles he had to endure from being denied access to dig sites, to disrespectful leaders who failed to honor his requests would've made any man quit, but Belzoni knew the only way to stand up to these bullies was to not give in to their demands.

There was a reason why Drovetti got so enraged seeing Belzoni discovering grandeur artifacts, opening beautiful tombs, and moving the colossi head: he was an engineer whose brain picked up on the ancient methods quicker than anyone else.

Lithograph of Fellahs hiding from Giovanni and Sarah Belzoni. Drawn and painted by Giovanni Belzoni

He was able to pinpoint where the tombs were located; how to remove the sands at Ybsambul and move the Memnon using the ancient Egyptian method of transportation. Drovetti was just too busy finding his next big score then appreciating the culture of Egypt. Does this make Belzoni an amateur? Of course not.

As German archaeologist Walter Wolf praises Belzoni's method. *"the typical representative of Egyptology in its heroic period, but his skill, intuition, and determination gave the world marvelous objects that were thought to have been lost forever."* So why does Belzoni continue to get treated not as an Egyptologist, but nothing more as a raider?

Modern archaeologists like to point out how Belzoni's raiding robbed the people of Egypt of their culture, their heritage, and above all, their history; however, the Fellahs of Egypt didn't care about the past. During the centuries they were occupied, they tore down the ancient monuments for housing material; with going as far as blowing the nose off the Sphinx!

Figure sketch of Giovanni Belzoni in Arabic dress

They knew if they found an artifact, they could sell it off to any European and make quick money. It wasn't till the mid to late nineteenth century when the science of modern archaeology and Egyptology began to take shape and the ideals of persevering Egyptian culture for future generations to admire and respect came to be.

Even the renowned archaeologist Howard Carter described Belzoni as *"one of the most remarkable men in the whole history of Egyptology,"* and further elaborated*:* *"This was the first occasion on which excavations on a large scale had ever been made in The Valley, and we must give Belzoni full credit for the manner in which they were carried out. There are episodes which give the modern excavator rather a shock, as, for example, when lie describes his method of dealing with sealed doorways - by means of a battering ram - but on the whole, the work was extraordinarily good."*

The Egypt Exploration Society (EES) in their *Famous Who Was Who in Egyptology*, praised Belzoni as the first pioneer of Egyptology:

William Flinders Petrie

The modern science of archaeology began with one man, William Flinders Petrie. Born in Kent in 1853, Petrie's life was intertwined with the ancient world. During his teenage years, Petrie surveyed the prehistoric monoliths known as Stonehenge and produced the most accurate planned that is still used today. In 1880, Petrie left his native home of England and ventured to Egypt for the first time.

The purpose for Petrie's trip to Egypt was to accurately measure the Great Pyramid of Khufu while disproving a theory proposed by a man named Piazzi Smyth in his book *Our Inheritance in the Great Pyramid*, that it wasn't the Egyptians intellect that built the pyramids but was the gods who divined to them how to build the pyramids. He based his theory on a system of measurement called the "pyramid inch".

Petrie spent the first two seasons in Egypt in an abandoned tomb on the Giza Plateau. Here, Petrie shared his new home with rats and fleas while awakening from the barks of wild dogs, but instead of complaining, Petrie found solace. *"Life here is really comfortable, without many of the encumbrances of regular hours: bells, collars, and cuffs, blacking, tablecloths, or many of the other unnecessaries of Civilization."* Within two years, Petrie disproved Smyth's pyramid inch as nothing more than pure fantasy. Petrie's survey was so accurate that is still used today amongst Egyptologists as the golden standard for future pyramid studies.

In 1883, his survey was published in *The Pyramid and Temples of Giza*, which alerted the newly formed *Egypt Exploration Fund* (EEF) to give the young English lad the chance of a lifetime: to travel through the Nile Delta and lead excavations. He became the first excavator to excavate San el-Hagar (the ancient Hyksos city of Tanis) and discovered the Greek trading center known as Naukratis. It was during these excavations that the modern science of archaeology came to be.

During excavations, Petrie would carefully observe pots that the Arabic workers later dubbed him *"Father of Pots"*. Petrie believed that pots were just as important as any mummy in a tomb; that they tell the story of the culture of ancient Egypt. This new method would take days or even years to complete; however, Petrie deemed it essential to take things slower. Why did he take this so seriously? Petrie believed it would protect the sites and monuments from damages.

    Petrie observed and recorded everything in mundane detail. His methods are still used today amongst Egyptologists and archaeologists. It's important that these ancient sites are preserved, protected, and given utmost respect for future generations to enjoy. One of the enduring impacts Petrie would have on Egypt was taking under his wing a young Howard Carter who would go on to study and utilize Petrie's methods to discover his tombs, but more importantly, it was Petrie's methods that allowed Carter to unearth the greatest tomb in the Valley of the Kings, the boy king, Tutankhamun on November 22, 1922.

(top) The *'Father of Pots'* William Flinders Petrie. (bottom) Howard Carter, discoverer of Pharaoh Tutankhamun.

Print of Giovanni Belzoni amongst his many discoveries (the Younger Memnon, the sarcophagus lid, the sarcophagi of Seti I, the head of Amenhotep III, and the statue of Setlios II

"He cannot be judged by the standards of later excavators such as Petrie, or even Mariette; but must be seen in the context of the period before decipherment; at the start of his career he was neither better nor worse than other contemporary figures, but he later evolved techniques for his work and acquired knowledge that raised him above the general level..."

It's a shame that many people today don't know who Giovanni Belzoni was and the extraordinary life he lived; however, in 1821, he was commemorated with a medal cast by Sir Edward Thomason.

    Giovanni is remembered more today as a tomb raider than an actual Egyptologist, but the spirit of Belzoni lives on. In 1981, Raiders of the Lost Ark made its way to theaters and captivated a new generation of history buffs. The film tells the story of Indiana Jones, part-time professor of archaeology and part-time adventurer, who is recruited by U.S. Intelligence to locate and retrieve the Ark of the Covenant- which houses the Ten Commandments of the Old Testament- before the Nazi's can get ahold of it and use it for world domination.

From there, Indiana Jones travels to Egypt, gets into near-death fights with Nazis, assassins, spies, goes on long goose chases to retrieve the Ark, raids an ancient tomb containing the Ark itself; all the while taking in the culture of 1930's Egypt. Sounds eerily to Giovanni Belzoni's time in Egypt, doesn't it? Both are raiders, getting into near-death fights and coming out of it with a new understanding and appreciation of the culture of the ancient past.

It's unclear if George Lucas, the creator of Star Wars, knew of Belzoni's existence when he was writing Raiders- he was mostly inspired by classic adventure films of the 1940's- but if he did, then it was honor worthy of the strongman himself. And speaking of Belzoni, what happened to Sarah after the death of her husband? When Giovanni died in December 1822, he left Sarah in financial straights. She tried and failed to put on exhibits of Belzoni's collection which resulted in increasing her financial problems. After spending years of campaigning, her friends- including the fabled author Charles Dickens- were given a 100-pound salary for the rest of her life. She died on January 12th, 1870 in the town of Jersey and was buried, alone and childless, with a simple gravestone.

Despite becoming the most famous man in London, Belzoni's achievements were overshadowed by Salt's collection of antiquities. Giovanni Belzoni, through all these faults and mishaps, was a painter who painted the world with his amazing discoveries. It's the painter we remember, not the man who commissioned it (in this case Mr. Salt) and shouldn't be punished for not following the correct methods of excavation, but instead, be admired for the accomplishments he made. Belzoni's collection would go on to become permanent members of the British Museum. Today, the British Museum's Egyptian gallery is coated by the discoveries of this adventurous man, the gentle giant from Padua.

Painted portrait of Giovanni Belzoni in Arabic garb with the Great Pyramid in the background.

Bibliography

Awed, Adel Zahraa & Dunn, Jimmy. *"Muhamad Ali Pasha"*- Tour Egypt. www.touregypt.net August 2020

Belzoni, Battista Giovanni. *Narrative of the Operations and Recent Discoveries Within the Pyramids, Temples, Tombs, and Excavations, in Egypt and Nubia And of a Journey to the Coast of the Red Sea in Search of the Ancient Berenice and Another to the Oasis of Jupiter Ammon.* 1822. Print

Bosworth, E.C. *"Henry Salt, Consul in Egypt 1816-1827 AND Pioneer of Egypt."* www.escholar.machester.ac.uk August 2020

Brier, Bob. *Egyptian Mummies: Unraveling the Secrets of an Ancient Art*. William Morrow and Company, Inc. New York. 1994.

Clayton, A. Peter. *Chronicle of The Pharaohs.* London: Thames and Hudson, 1994.Print

Fairfax, Ferdinand. *"Egypt: The Pharaoh and the Showman."* Perf. Matthew Kelly. BBC. Docudrama. 2005

Fairfax, Ferdinand. *"Egypt: The Temple of the Sands."* Perf. Matthew Kelly. BBC. Docudrama. 2005

"Giovanni Battista Belzoni- Ancient Egypt and Archaeology." February 27, 2020. www.ancient.co.uk August 2020

Hayhurst, Mark. *"Seekers of the Lost Treasure- The Great Belzoni."* Perf. Jeremey Irons. Discovery Networks. Documentary. www.youtube.com July 2020

Heath, Julian. *Archaeology Hotspot Egypt: Unearthing the Past for Armchair Archaeologists.* Maryland: Rowman & Littlefield, 2015.

Madden, April. *"All About History: Book of Ancient Egypt."* London: Future Publishing Ltd, 2017. Print

Mikics, David. *"Percy Bysshe Shelly: 'Ozymandias'.* Poetry Foundation. March 11, 2020. www.poetryfoundation.org August 2020

National Geographic. *Essential Visual History of The Bible.* National Geographic Society. Washington, DC. 2008

Parsons, Marie. *"Giovanni Belzoni Circus Giant And Collector of Egyptian Antiquities."* www.touregypt.net August 2020

Reeves, Nicholas & Wilkinson, H. Richard. *The Complete Valley of the Kings: Tombs and Treasures of Egypt's Greatest Pharaohs.* London: Thames & Hudson. 1996

'*Robinson Crusoe: Summary, Characters & Facts.*' www.britannica.com August 2020

Strudwick, Helen. *The Encyclopedia of Ancient Egypt.* New York: Metro Books, 2006.

Teodorani, Arnaldo. *"Giovanni Battista Belzoni- A Real-Life Indiana Jones."* Perf. Simon Whistler. Biographics. Documentary. May 13, 2019. www.youtube.com July 2020

"The Mali Empire." Resource Library. August, 20, 2020. www.nationalgeographic.org September 2020

Tyldesley, Joyce. *The Pharaohs.* Great Britain: Quercus Editions, 2009.

Webster, David. *"Giovanni Belzoni: Strongman Archaeologist."* European Corner: Iron Game History Vol. 1 Number 2, 1990. Starkcenter.org August 2020

Wilkinson, Toby. *The Rise and Fall of Ancient Egypt.* New York: Random House, INC. 2010.

Wills, Henry William. *"The Story of Giovanni Belzoni." Household Words, Volume II Magazine No. 49* March 1851. www.lalampadina.net August 2020

Photo References

Category: Images-Wikimedia Commons.
commons.wikimedia.org

Operations of G. Belzoni In Egypt and Nubia.
www.rawpixel.com

Rosicrucian Egyptian Museum. San Jose, CA

Travis "T.J." Frank has always been fascinated by history, but more importantly, the men and women who made history. When he learned about Egypt at an early age did his passion for history emerge. He is the author of *Akhenaten: Egypt's Mysterious Pharaoh*. He has a BA in history and currently resides in California

Printed by Amazon Italia Logistica S.r.l.
Torrazza Piemonte (TO), Italy